CLO INVESTING

CLO Investing: with an Emphasis on CLO Equity & BB Notes

Copyright © 2023 by Shiloh Bates

Library of Congress Control Number: 2023942353

ISBN (paperback): 9781642376562

Collateralized Loan Obligations (CLOs) were left for dead after the Global Financial Crisis ("GFC") of 2008-2009. But, since then, CLOs have made a surprising comeback. Their popularity among investors is partially the result of their performance during the GFC and beyond. CLO Notes issued before the GFC did not have material defaults. And many CLO equity securities issued prior to the GFC ended up with annualized returns above 20%. Today the CLO market has over $1 trillion in assets under management and has replaced banks as the largest lender to private equity-backed companies.

This book describes CLOs in detail, emphasizing CLO BB Notes and Equity, the securities with the highest risk and reward potential. The reader will learn the characteristics of the CLO's leveraged loans, its financing structure, payment rules and tests, and historical returns. Strategies for investing in these securities are also discussed in detail.

As CLOs are gaining in popularity, investment professionals of all varieties will benefit from understanding this unique market.

Table of Contents

Introduction 1

    1.1 CLO Basics 1

    1.2 Primary CLO Investing Strategies 9

A CLO's Leveraged loans.. 11

    2.1 Leveraged Loan Overview 11

    2.2 Basics of Leveraged Loan Credit Analysis 16

    2.3 EBITDA Add-backs.. 20

    2.4 Financial Covenants 23

    2.5 Loan Documentation 24

    2.6 Loan Amendments 25

    2.7 Credit Underwriting Process..................................... 26

    2.8 Borrower Projection Model....................................... 30

    2.9 Leveraged Loan Monitoring...................................... 32

    2.10 Historical Loan Defaults and Recoveries................. 35

    2.11 Historical Loan Returns 40

CLO Participants... 45

    3.1 CLO Manager 45

    3.2 CLO Arranger... 52

    3.3 Rating Agencies.. 54

    3.4 CLO Trustee... 67

CLO Financing Structure.. 68

    4.1 The Simplified Bank 68

    4.2 Overcollateralization Tests....................................... 73

    4.3 Interest Coverage Tests... 77

4.4 Collateral Quality Tests 77

4.5 Market Value Analytics 81

4.6 Loan Loss Reserve.. 83

4.7 Fixed Rate Tranches... 85

4.8 The X Note.. 86

4.9 The Fee Rebate Letter 87

Interest Rates **89**

5.1 Transition to SOFR 91

5.2 LIBOR/SOFR Basis 92

CLO Key Terms **94**

6.1 Documentation 94

6.2 Indenture Amendments... 94

6.3 Refinancings and Resets... 95

6.4 Par Flush.. 99

6.5 Reinvestment After the End of the Reinvestment
Period... 101

Warehousing..**104**

7.1 Warehouse Overview.. 104

7.2 Warehouse Returns Model...................................... 106

7.3 Print and Sprint CLO Formations 108

Self-Healing..**109**

8.1 Loan Gains in Distressed Times 109

8.2 Self-Healing Forward Projections............................. 110

8.3 Self-Healing Historical Case Study........................... 113

Flavors of CLOs **114**

9.1 CLO 1.0 and 2.0... 114

9.2 Static CLOs 115

9.3 Middle Market CLOs.. 117

9.4 Insurance Company Optimized CLOs............................. 122
9.5 Excess CCC/Caa CLOs... 123
9.6 Balance Sheet CLOs... 125

CLO Modeling **126**

10.1 Simplified CLO Model 126
10.2 Detailed CLO Model in Excel 127
10.3 CLO Modeling Using Third-Party Software 131
10.4 Critical Nature of Correct CLO Equity Modeling........ 133

CLO Equity Investing... **135**

11.1 Sourcing CLO Equity 135
11.2 CLO Auction Process 138
11.3 Market Tracking.. 139

Historical Equity Returns **147**

12.1 IRRs for CLOs by Vintage................................ 147
12.2 Negative IRR CLO Equity................................. 149
12.3 CLO Equity Index 150
12.4 CLO Equity Highest Returns............................. 153

CLO BB Notes.. **155**

13.1 CLO BB Basics... 155
13.2 CLO BB Returns... 157
13.3 CLO BB Structural Features 158
13.4 CLO BB Note Default Rate............................... 161
13.5 CLO BB Note Investment Strategies...................... 163
13.6 Par Subordination 164
13.7 Market Value Over Collateralization...................... 165
13.8 Discount Margin 166
13.9 BB Note Trading... 168
13.10 B Notes 171

Common Mistakes in CLO Investing 173

    14.1 Lessons Learned 173

Market Participant Perspectives 176

    15.1 Drew Sweeney, TCW, Broadly Syndicated
    Loan Manager 176
    15.2 Kelli Marti, Churchill Asset Management,
    Middle Market CLO Manager 179
    15.3 Chris Gilbert, Natixis, CLO Arranger 185
    15.4 Brad Larson, Credit Suisse, CLO Arranger 194

Conclusion 200

Glossary 201

Introduction

1.1 CLO Basics

In 1998, I started my finance career as an investment banking analyst at First Union Securities, now part of Wells Fargo. One of my first assignments was arranging a financing for a Collateralized Loan Obligation (CLO) manager. At the time, I had never heard of a CLO. Two years later, the same CLO manager hired me to pick leveraged loans for its CLOs.

Back then, there was less than $20 billion of annual CLO issuance and only a handful of CLO managers. It was truly a backwater of finance. However, during my career, CLO assets under management have grown rapidly. As of year-end 2022, there were over 120 managers issuing CLOs in a $1 trillion asset class.

Annual Issuance of New U.S. CLOs ($ Billions)

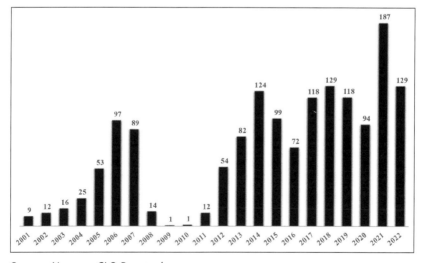

Source: Nomura CLO Research

Diversified pools of leveraged loans are the assets of a CLO. Most leveraged loans are created in a Leveraged Buyout (LBO), where a private equity firm buys a company. Half of the purchase price may be paid for with equity, while the remainder may be financed with a leveraged loan. The leveraged loan is senior and secured, has a floating rate, and is rated below investment grade by rating agencies.

Investors find leveraged loans attractive for a few reasons. First, they offer attractive current income, usually around 3.5% over a floating rate of the London Interbank Offer Rate (LIBOR) or the Secured Overnight Funding Rate (SOFR). Second, they default rarely, and if they default, the leveraged loan owners usually recoup two-thirds of their money. Third, and key to this book, is that lenders will extend favorable terms to finance diversified pools of leveraged loans.

Few people would want to own one loan, even if it's made to a great company. The reason is considerable downside risk if something negative affects the business. Investors prefer pools of leveraged loans because diversification reduces risk. In a diversified portfolio, some leveraged loans will likely default, but income from the other loans should enable the overall loan portfolio to generate a favorable return.

A CLO's structure resembles a simplified bank. It allows investors to get exposure to first lien senior secured loans, but on a leveraged basis. A CLO uses securitization technology to divide the cash flows received from the pool of leveraged loans according to agreed-upon rules.

Assets	**Liabilities and Equity**
First Lien Loans	AAA Notes
Floating Rate	
Secured by Assets of the Company	
Private Equity-Owned Borrowers	AA Notes
	A Notes
	BBB Notes
	BB Notes
	CLO Equity

Many CLOs issued today have expected lives of eight or more years. Tranches are the different portions of the CLO's financing that have ratings from AAA down to equity. The CLO's cost of debt is locked in for the life of a CLO. However, the CLO's equity investors have the option to refinance specific CLO tranches at more favorable rates after the end of a non-call period, typically two years. The equity tranche is the most subordinated one and is not rated.

CLO equity offers the potential for mid-teens returns with a low correlation to other asset classes, such as stocks or high yield bonds. In contrast to other alternative investments, there is no "J Curve" in CLO equity, meaning you can start recouping your initial investment quickly. That's because CLOs pay quarterly distributions, and the initial distributions can be in the mid-teens percent or better. The high initial cash flows mitigate the investment risk and make it harder—though not impossible—to have a negative lifetime Internal Rate of Return (IRR).

The CLO equity investor will bear the losses when any leveraged loans in the CLO default. Fortunately, the 30 years of default and recovery history in the leveraged loan asset class can apply some bounds on potential loan losses in the CLO. Each year the loss rate on leveraged loans varies and is a function of overall US economic conditions combined with trends in particular industries in which the CLO has invested.

A potential downside to CLO equity is volatility, which can be equity-like in some market environments. While investment banks will make a market in CLO equity, the bid-ask spread can be wide. As a result, it's best to think of CLO equity as a long-term investment.

An investor in CLO BB Notes may target a low double-digit return while taking less risk than the CLO equity investors. The BB Note investors have a secured interest in the leveraged loans in the CLO, but they sit behind more senior noteholders in payment priority. The CLO BB Note investor benefits from the initial equity contributed to the CLO, which takes the first loss on the underlying leveraged loans. Additionally, if loans owned by the CLO deteriorate in credit quality, it's possible to redirect the CLO's profitability from the equity tranche to benefit the CLO's noteholders.

During the 2008-2009 Global Financial Crisis ("GFC"), CLO issuance dried up for almost three years. To the surprise of many, it turned out that CLOs issued before the GFC performed well on a buy-and-hold basis. Returns were aided by what is referred to as the CLO's "self-healing mechanism." Chapter 8 of this book will describe how it works in detail.

CLOs have historically been an asset only available to large institutional investors. Given what I believe are the attractive risk/return characteristics of CLOs and CLO equity and BB

Notes in particular, I believe retail investors will increasingly want access to the asset class. This is especially true because many economists are predicting long-term annualized equity returns of 5–7%.

CLOs issued today have little in common with the Collateralized Debt Obligations (CDOs) issued before the financial crisis. Many of those CDOs—featured in the book, *The Big Short,* by Michael Lewis, were backed by subprime mortgage loans of dubious quality. Securitization is a powerful tool, and the results can be favorable when quality assets are securitized, and leverage is applied on appropriate terms and levels. The association of today's CLOs with the failed CDOs of the past is one of the reasons that investors in CLOs can earn an excess return above comparable risk assets.

Item	CLOs	CDOs
Underlying Collateral	Senior secured corporate loans	Mezzanine tranches, high grade ABS tranches, subprime mortgages
Transparency	Detailed monthly reporting including all loans, purchases, sales, loan ratings, and prices	Reporting generally did not link to underlying assets
Management	Actively managed by some of the largest US asset management firms	Static and managed portfolio of securitizations
Correlation of underlying assets	CLOs are required to have a diverse portfolio across industries and borrowers	Highly correlated to home prices
Returns	Favorable returns for the equity tranche	Defaults on investment grade tranches

While there are many investors in a CLO, the CLO equity investor runs the show. He or she will pick the CLO manager and the CLO arranger (the investment bank that brings the CLO to life). While investors in the CLO Notes will have a significant say in the CLO's formation, if the CLO equity investor isn't happy with the outcome, the CLO will not form. The initial BB Note investors are usually some of the last participants to commit to the CLO. Their tranche size is small as a % of the CLO's funding. The BB Note upside is capped because the maximum final payout is par value. The BB Note investors are often primarily focused on only a few key CLO terms.

Many financial firms have gotten into trouble because their assets are of longer duration than their liabilities. The banking crisis of spring 2023 is one prescient example. If the assets are illiquid and the financing market isn't open when liabilities come due, it's a big problem. CLOs are structured with financing longer than the expected life of all the CLO's leveraged loans. There should never be a time when a CLO is a forced seller of assets in a depressed market.

Just as no two snowflakes are alike, no two CLOs are either. Their differences reflect market conditions at the time of CLO formation and the relative needs of the investors in the CLO. This heterogeneity enables CLO equity investors to express their differing market views and try to earn excess returns in what is an inefficient asset class. Without the many nuances of different CLO structures, there wouldn't be the need for so many CLO investment analysts like me.

A CLO BB Note is usually the junior-most debt tranche in the CLO. Its investors target high-single-digit/low-teens returns and expect that the performance of the underlying CLO leveraged loans will be adequate to fully repay the tranche at the end of the CLO's life. The CLO BB Note might have an initial 12-year maturity, but investors expect that the BB Note will be repaid much sooner than that.

CLO BB Notes usually benefit from a minimum of 8% equity that takes the first loss when any of the CLO's loans default. If the equity amount is positive at the end of the CLO's life, the CLO BB Note is repaid at par.

If the CLO's collateral quality deteriorates with CCC/Caa-rated leveraged loans or defaults over prescribed limits, the CLO will stop making distributions to the equity. Instead, cash that would have otherwise gone to the equity is retained in the CLO and used to buy more loans or repay the AAA tranche. Because CLO equity investors target mid-teens returns, a significant amount of cash could potentially be diverted for the benefit of the CLO BB and other CLO debt tranches.

The typical lifecycle for a CLO with a five-year reinvestment period looks like this:

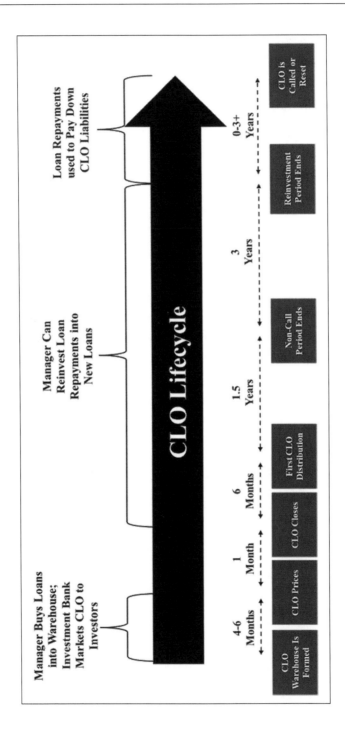

Before the CLO is created, a warehouse facility is formed to acquire leveraged loans for the CLO. On the CLO pricing date, the CLO's financing is arranged. Trade tickets are distributed to all the CLO's investors. There is a month before the CLO's financing closes. That gives the CLO additional time to add to the leveraged loan portfolio. When the CLO is mostly done investing its portfolio, the CLO goes effective. That's when the rating agencies confirm their ratings and the CLO's tests begin being measured. CLOs make their distributions quarterly, but usually, the first payment will come with a lag as the CLO is likely not fully invested at closing. Two years into the CLO's life, the non-call period on the CLO's debt ends, and CLO equity investors can begin making equity-accretive changes to the CLO's financing. At the end of the five-year reinvestment period, the CLO will begin deleveraging as prepayments are received from the leveraged loans. The deleveraging process ends when the equity investors decide to call the CLO.

1.2 Primary CLO Investing Strategies

CLO equity and BB Notes are sold to accredited investors and qualified institutional buyers with over $100 million of assets under management. They're usually not sold directly to individuals. Investment banks are leery of selling CLO securities directly to retail investors because if the investment doesn't work out as expected, the retail investor may claim that they were misled into making the investment.

There isn't a way to invest in CLO equity or BB Notes in the same way an investor can get exposure to the S&P 500 index by buying an exchange-traded fund with minimal management fees.

When I first started investing in CLO equity, I visited two top-tier CLO managers to conduct due diligence and determine which CLO equity I should buy. Both firms had impressive offices in Midtown Manhattan, large credit teams, and substantial firm resources outside of CLOs. Upon returning to my office, I found it difficult to distinguish between the two firms. After pondering the question for a few days, I realized that I wouldn't be able to know which of the firms would do a better job in selecting the CLO's leveraged loans. However, one of the CLOs was being offered with economics more favorable to the equity than the other, and that's the investment I chose. Then I developed a framework to distill the 120 CLO managers into a top quartile. Within the top quartile, I have only a handful of strong preferences. Sticking to the top quartile managers, my goal is to buy CLO equity with the most favorable returns for the equity. Surprising to many, when a CLO is created, the CLO equity is often sold to different investors at different prices. And the secondary market for CLO equity is quite inefficient.

The second part of the investment strategy is determining the profile of the CLO equity I'm interested in buying. This is partially dictated by the returns I'm seeking and the risk I'm willing to take. Many CLO equity investors will gravitate towards buying CLO equity in newly-issued CLOs. Arrangers would be happy to walk investors through that process. However, this is often not where the best returns are found.

I take a different strategy for investing in CLO BB Notes, which have exceptionally low historical default rates. For these investments, managers outside of the top quartile may be of interest. That's because their debt costs are higher, and often, there are additional structural protections for the CLO Note investors. CLO BB Notes in newly created CLOs are all sold at the same price. But in the secondary market, investors may purchase these securities at more attractive prices than other market participants.

A CLO's Leveraged loans

2.1 Leveraged Loan Overview

The assets of a typical CLO include $500 million of first lien senior secured loans. The CLO's leveraged loans are extremely diversified, with 200+ leveraged loans to distinct companies. Standard and Poor's ("S&P") and Moody's Investors Service ("Moody's") rate the leveraged loans at B/B2 on average. The CLO's levered loans pay interest on a floating rate based on the LIBOR or SOFR plus a spread. As SOFR leveraged loan issuance began in 2022, few leveraged loans were SOFR-based as of December 2022.

Below are a few companies that have loans in CLOs. In total, these kinds of companies have borrowed more than $1.3 trillion.

- Asurion
- Cablevision Systems
- TransDigm
- Altice France
- CenturyLink
- Virgin Media
- Univision Communications
- Amneal Pharmaceuticals
- Starfruit Finco B.V.
- United Continental Holdings

Given the diversity of leveraged loans in a CLO, an investor could own less than 10 CLOs and have exposure to over 1,000 leveraged loans. CLOs managed by different CLO managers usually have lower overlap on the leveraged loans, while CLOs managed by the same asset manager may own similar loan portfolios. Usually, a CLO manager will invest in a new leveraged loan and divide its purchase into all the CLOs it manages, or at least those CLOs that have the cash to deploy. While there are hundreds of leveraged loans in a CLO, the few that default will play a large role in differentiating the returns of one CLO's equity tranche from those of another.

The Volcker Rule, implemented in 2013, essentially prohibited CLOs from owning high yield bonds. However, a repeal of the Volcker Rule made it possible for CLOs to own a small percentage of high yield bonds today. Typically, these bonds will be first lien secured.

The typical leveraged loan issuer in a CLO is owned by a private equity firm, also commonly referred to as a financial sponsor. Leveraged Buyouts (LBOs) have been around since the 1980s, with RJR Nabisco being one of the first notable deals in 1988.

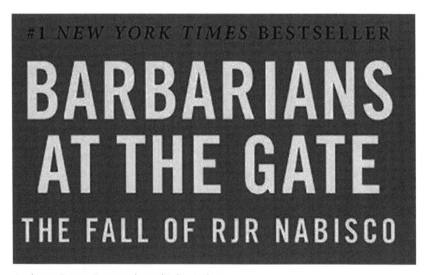

Authors: Bryan Burrough and John Helyar

According to Dealroom, the largest private equity firms in 2022 were:

1. BlackRock
2. Blackstone
3. Apollo Global Management
4. KKR
5. The Carlyle Group
6. CVC Capital Partners
7. TPG
8. Thoma Bravo
9. EQT
10. Insight Partners

When a private equity firm acquires a company, it usually contributes a portion of the purchase price—around 50%—in equity.

The firm usually finances the remainder of the LBO purchase price by issuing leveraged loans and high yield bonds. Private equity firms purchase companies they believe will grow revenue and profits over time and, thus, increase the value of their equity investment. The use of leverage amplifies the returns private equity firms expect to earn. Of course, the leverage will work against them if the returns are negative. Private equity firms hire investment banks to arrange debt financings for the companies they buy. JP Morgan, Citigroup, and BAML, for example, earn an underwriting fee to place a leveraged loan with various investors, including CLOs. The leveraged loans are referred to as "broadly syndicated" because each loan will have numerous participating lenders/investors. Sometimes the arranging bank will keep some of the leveraged loans on its balance sheet, and other times it becomes entirely owned by third parties. Today CLOs are the largest investor in broadly syndicated leveraged loans, at more than 75% market share. Loan mutual funds, alternative asset managers, Business Development Companies (BDCs), and hedge funds also invest in leveraged loans.

When the bank agrees to underwrite a leveraged loan, there are usually a few months between when that commitment is made and when the leveraged loan will be sold to the investors. However, CLOs will buy loans at the prices available in the current market. They do not make the forward financing commitments that banks do. If the market conditions change for the worse, as they did in 2022, it's the banks that take the loss, not CLOs.

Photo: Ken Wolter/Shutterstock.com

Citrix Debt Deal Prices with Large Loss for Banks

Sale of cloud-computing company's debt has been closely watched by private equity investors

---

Source: Wall Street Journal, September 21, 2022

Issuance of leveraged loans varies each year, with more issuance in years when the economy is on solid footing. In recessionary years, investors in leveraged loans will want higher returns, and many companies will decide to put any new financing plans on hold.

From the investment bank's perspective, earning an underwriting fee without having much capital at risk in the form of a leveraged loan is ideal. It enables a bank to maximize its return on equity, a key metric for bank investors. Additionally, a bank would generally not want to lend hundreds of millions to one company, regardless of the company's business prospects. That's because the bank would have a substantial hole in its balance sheet, if the loan went bad.

At the end of 2022, many leveraged loans in CLOs paid a base rate of 4.75% for LIBOR, plus a 3.50% spread for an 8.25% total yield. Leveraged loans often have LIBOR or SOFR floors of 0.50% to 1.0%. If the base rate drops below the floor, the base rate will be the floor. This provides income protection for the leveraged loan investor if the base rate drops significantly. New-issue leveraged loans are usually bought at a slight discount to par (0.5% to 1.0%) further increasing returns for the leveraged loan investor.

Usually, leveraged loans have amortization (mandatory payments) of 1% per year, with the remainder due at maturity. Some loans allow for borrowing on a revolving basis, but these are not frequently found in CLOs. Some loans will have delayed-draw features that allow the borrower to draw the loan in the future for uses like approved acquisitions. However, CLOs usually prefer to own leveraged loans that are initially fully funded because the CLO needs to reserve a cash balance for unfunded assets. Having CLO investments in cash is not accretive to the CLO's returns.

Investment banks buy and sell broadly syndicated leveraged loans in the secondary market. Some loans are over $1 billion and trade frequently in the secondary market. Other loans are $250 million in size and trade infrequently. The smaller loans generally have marginally higher interest rates to compensate investors for their lack of liquidity. Investment banks make a spread of around

50 basis points, or "bps," of the loan's principal balance if it's frequently traded.

Although a typical broadly syndicated loan has a stated maturity of five to seven years, these loans frequently prepay as there are minimal penalties for doing so. A newly issued broadly syndicated loan today might have a six-month period in which the borrower would pay a 50 bps fee if the leveraged loan is refinanced. Otherwise, the loan would be pre-payable at par. The typical broadly syndicated loan is only outstanding for around three years. The chief financial officers of the borrowers in the CLO are risk-averse individuals; they don't like to have near-term debt maturities because the debt markets aren't always open. Prepayments can arise when the debt is refinanced with other debt or when the company is sold.

2.2 Basics of Leveraged Loan Credit Analysis

Firms that invest in leveraged loans have an investment team that extensively researches the leveraged loan before it's purchased. The financial analysts who do this work often have previous commercial or investment banking experience and have earned an MBA or Chartered Financial Analyst® designation. While credit analysis is outside this book's scope, the basics are outlined below.

Loan-to-Value

A starting point is usually a comparison of the amount of the leveraged loan to the value of the entire business. This metric is called loan-to-value. The trick is that most of the businesses are not publicly traded, so the financial analyst needs to consider the most recent purchase price and comparable historical transactions for similar businesses. An investor in leveraged loans will want a low loan-to-value so that if the business' enterprise value deteriorates, he or she will still be repaid. Conversely, the private equity firm that owns the business prefers a high loan-to-value, which requires less equity to finance the business. In 2022, an initial loan-to-value in the leveraged loan market was 40% to 60%. When the loan-to-value is higher, the investor in the leveraged loan will require a premium spread over LIBOR/SOFR as extra compensation for the risk he or she is taking. For the leveraged loan investor, the best thing that can happen is for the loan to make all its contractual interest and principal payments. If the business grows, as its private equity firm's owner might expect, the leveraged loan investor does not participate in the upside. The leveraged loan investor takes the risk that the business' performance declines significantly, and contractual interest and principal payments are not met. When this happens, the business files for bankruptcy, and the leveraged loans are likely impaired. Historically this has happened to fewer than 3% of companies annually in the broadly syndicated loan market since 1992, according to JP Morgan Research.

Leverage Multiple

Besides loan-to-value, an investor in leveraged loans must consider the company's leverage multiple. A company's Earnings Before Interest, Taxes, Depreciation, and Amortization (EBITDA) is used as a proxy for annual cash generation. EBITDA is then compared to the amount of debt outstanding, usually net of any cash on the borrower's balance sheet.

Typical LBO Financing

A higher leverage multiple implies more risk for the lender and less equity cushion in the business. A typical broadly syndicated loan has 4.5 times its EBITDA in total debt, including first lien loans, second lien loans, and high yield bonds. The market leverage multiple varies over time, with recessionary periods pushing the multiple higher because EBITDA declines or because the borrowers use more leverage.

An investor in leveraged loans might be okay with a higher leverage multiple for a business that is growing steadily and achieving increased profitability. In comparison, a lower leverage multiple would be appropriate for a cyclical company or one with less favorable business prospects. The interest rate will also be a factor—more leverage usually means a higher required spread over LIBOR/SOFR to compensate the lender for the increased risk. Most new-issue leveraged loans today have an initial first lien leverage of 3.0 to 6.0x EBITDA, a wide range driven by the factors discussed above.

Surprisingly to some, a CLO manager can make a "good" loan to a "bad" company if structured correctly. For example, a "bad" company might be in a cyclical industry with low profit margins. However, some combination of low leverage, high loan spread, and financial covenants could result in an attractive loan.

Interest Coverage Ratio

Higher interest rates benefit investors in leveraged loans, provided that the borrower has the financial capacity to make the payments. At the end of 2021, many loans covered their interest with a ratio of 5.0x EBITDA, near all-time highs.

However, LIBOR increased dramatically in 2022 and was projected to increase further into 2023. A way to assess a borrower's ability to make interest payments in the higher LIBOR environment is shown below. If LIBOR peaks at 5.0%, as current interest rate markets predict, the interest coverage ratio is expected to decline from 5.0 to 2.9x EBITDA. It's a sharp decline, but interest coverage over 2.0x EBITDA is usually considered healthy. Of course, cash flow could become tight for borrowers more levered than in my example below.

	12/31/2021	Peak Libor
Loan Amount ($ in millions)	1,000	1,000
Spread over LIBOR	3.50%	3.50%
LIBOR	1.00%	5.00%
Leverage	4.00x	4.00x
EBITDA ($ in millions)	250	250
Interest Expense ($ in millions)	45	85
Interest Coverage	5.6x	2.9x

The forward LIBOR curve was downward sloping beginning in the summer of 2023, which could provide some relief to higher interest payments.

2.3 EBITDA Add-backs

If you ask several credit analysts what a company's leverage multiple is, you may get different results! Generally, there would be a consensus about the debt level, though some credit analysts would include long-term leases in with long-term debt. However, many credit analysts would have different adjusted EBITDA numbers.

EBITDA is the key cash flow metric for leveraged loan analysis. However, EBITDA, as calculated from a company's audited financial statements, often must be adjusted to a true run-rate basis.

Adjusted EBITDA starts with net income and adds back interest, taxes, depreciation, and amortization, as noted above. Let's say a business has generated $100 million of EBITDA for the previous year, but the business recently lost one of its largest customers. In this scenario, we will not be lending off the $100 million EBITDA number. Instead, we will adjust the EBITDA downward to better capture the run-rate or future EBITDA level.

Adjusted EBITDA also includes other add-backs for certain expenses, such as owner-related excess compensation or above-market rent to a building controlled by the owner, which an acquirer is unlikely to pay going forward. Running personal expenses through the company is quite common in family-owned businesses. These expenses can include club dues, owner automobile expenses, excessive travel, meals and entertainment, and family members on the payroll who may not contribute much to the business and will not continue to work there going forward.

Below is a list of common EBITDA adjustments found in leveraged loans. These adjustments are usually derived from two sources: (1) discussions with the management team and the company's third-party advisors; and (2) detailed forensic analysis by the buyer's advisor, typically a consulting firm such as Alvarez & Marsal or L.E.K. Consulting.

- Owner-related excess compensation
- Professional fees, such as legal fees related to a transaction
- Non-recurring income (which would be deducted from EBITDA)
- Rent expense to a related-party real estate entity
- Retirement plan expenses to the owner or owner-related staff who will not be employed post-transaction
- Former owner consulting expenses
- Inventory normalization
- Bad debt, payroll accrual, bonus, and payroll tax normalization

In addition to the EBITDA adjustments above, it's common for companies to look at potential synergies in the future and add a run-rate figure to the current EBITDA. If the transaction involves consolidating two businesses, there typically would be manufacturing and other operational synergies projected to be realized within 12 to 18 months and included in the current EBITDA figure. Cost-saving actions such as headcount rationalization, team rightsizing, or offshoring are also factored in. An analyst must conduct proper due diligence on these forward-looking synergies and cost savings that are included in the adjusted EBITDA figure. The analyst must also haircut in a conservative estimation of what he or she deems to be a solid, recurring level of annual EBITDA. Quite often, these cost savings and synergies take longer than expected to be realized, or never reach their projected amounts.

Below is a list of some examples of synergy and cost-saving actions. Cost savings are quite often broken out into headcount and non-headcount categories. Generally, the headcount actions are easier to quantify and more quickly realized. A transaction is viewed more favorably if most cost savings are headcount related.

- Team right-sizing
- Selected offshoring and/or increased outsourcing
- Function deduplication/harmonization
- Standardizing service-level agreements across the combined entity
- Recalibration of product management
- Consolidation of overlapping customer base
- Reduction of non-customer-facing roles
- Exit de-emphasized markets/products

These savings and synergies come with a cost that should be factored into the projected synergies and cost savings. Management will estimate the cost to achieve the expected headcount reductions or operational efficiencies. The general rule with headcount reductions is that the cost of attaining them represents approximately half of the desired savings target.

In general, seeing EBITDA adjustments represent less than 20% of the total EBITDA figure is favorable. If EBITDA adjustments approach 30% or higher, additional diligence is warranted, and more granular details should be requested.

While EBITDA add-backs may sound like a technicality, whether add-backs are accepted plays a significant role in whether a leveraged loan will be bought or not. Let's say a credit analyst believes all the add-backs, then leverage might be at 4.5x EBITDA, an appropriate level. But if the add-backs are not accepted, adjusted EBITDA is lower, and leverage might be 5.5x. At that leverage level, the loan might be declined.

2.4 Financial Covenants

Some loans will have financial covenants that require a borrower to have a minimum level of EBITDA compared to the amount of money borrowed. Another common financial covenant is a test that compares the company's EBITDA to the amount of annual interest expense. A violation of a financial covenant is considered a default under the leveraged loan's legal documentation, even though the company may not have missed an interest or principal payment. If these covenants are not part of the leveraged loan documentation, the loan is covenant-lite.

There has been a steady increase in the issuance of covenant-lite loans in the United States, and today around 80% of broadly syndicated loans are covenant-lite. The trend reflects a more borrower-friendly loan market, where many lenders want to deploy significant amounts of capital.

Most loans have negative covenants, which mandate that the business cannot enter into any arrangement that would reduce the borrower's credit quality. Examples include limitations on acquisitions, additional borrowings, or the sale of certain assets.

While lenders prefer having financial covenants on the leveraged loans, a CLO pool that is mainly covenant-lite may have lower defaults over its life. That is because only a missed interest or principal payment can cause a default. There are examples of companies that have experienced sharp decreases in EBITDA that would have defaulted if covenants were present. Because they were not, the company managed to survive and recover. Ironically, if the leveraged loan had covenants, its lenders could have taken over the company and sold it to the highest bidder, resulting in a substantial loss in a down market. A lack of financial covenants on the loans can push a borrower's problems into the future, while the CLO's equity investors benefit from high current cash flows, especially at the beginning of the CLO's life.

2.5 Loan Documentation

The credit agreement of a leveraged loan is the legal document that governs the relationship between a lender and a borrower. This document, often over 200 pages in length, provides a detailed outline of the terms and conditions of the agreement. There are many critical features that lenders must carefully review before executing the agreement. Starting with some of the basics, the agreement designates the various parties to the agreement, including the borrower, the lead lender (agent), and the broader lender group, if applicable. Further, the document states the total amount of money that is being borrowed for the facility and the interest rate of the facility.

Default provisions are more nuanced. This section details what happens if the borrower violates any terms of the agreement, such as failing to make the required payments or breaching a financial covenant. In the event of default, the lender has a variety of rights and remedies, such as the right to increase the interest rate, the right to accelerate the loan's maturity, the right to take possession of certain collateral, or the right to sue the borrower for breach of contract. Another key feature of the loan documentation is the security of the loan. This is a detailed description of the borrower's collateral that is used to secure the loan. Though term loan lenders typically underwrite a loan with the expectation of being repaid via the borrower's cash flows, lenders also maintain a first lien on essentially all the assets of the borrower in case of a liquidation scenario. This includes the borrower's receivables, inventory, real estate, equipment and intellectual property, among other assets with quantifiable value. The restricted payments component of the agreement defines limited or prohibited types of payments, such as shareholder dividends, stock buybacks, early debt repayments, or transfers of cash and other assets to unrestricted subsidiaries that are not governed by the credit agreement. Lenders do not want the value of the collateral over which they hold a lien to be reduced. This is especially important when a borrower is financially distressed, as private equity firms may try to devise ways to extract equity value and recoup their investment by removing certain subsidiaries or other assets from the loan's collateral. Similarly, lenders also do not want private equity firms taking cash out of the business as dividends that would otherwise be used to pay down debt or support business operations to generate cash flow. Lenders also prefer that private equity firms maintain a vested financial interest in growing the business and improving its performance. Financial reporting requirements are another crucial aspect included in credit agreements. These requirements consist of quarterly unaudited financial statements throughout the fiscal year as well as audited annual financial statements. Calls hosted by management during which the lenders can ask questions about recent performance are often another requirement.

2.6 Loan Amendments

There are many reasons why a credit agreement might be amended. Some of the most common reasons would be to increase the size of the facility to allow for activities such as an acquisition, to permit the sale or release of certain assets from the collateral pool, to provide a temporary grace period from debt-service payments, or to avoid a potential covenant breach. If the business is not viewed as substantially impaired but rather suffered a bad quarter or two due to exogenous factors such as the COVID-19 pandemic, lenders and borrowers may proactively work together to avoid a covenant breach, given the potential legal and financial consequences to both parties. Certain amendments only require a majority of lenders to approve an amendment. However, credit agreements also include sacred rights provisions for which any changes require approval from 100% of the lender group. Due to sacred rights provisions, extensions to the loan's maturity, reductions to the interest rate, changes to the due dates of interest and principal payments, and increases or decreases in the size of the credit facility beyond the permitted additional indebtedness baskets require 100% lender approval to amend. In addition to providing flexibility or relief to the borrower, lenders may receive a one-time payment for approving an amendment. The amount varies, but 0.25% to 1.0% of each lender's respective outstanding principal balance is customary. For non-material amendments, the lenders may approve it without a fee.

2.7 Credit Underwriting Process

The typical credit approval process for a new primary loan transaction involves several steps, including a pre-screen, an initial investment committee screen, due diligence activities, and ongoing dialogue with the agent bank leading the transaction. These steps lead to a full investment committee meeting where a decision is made on whether to approve the leveraged loan for investment by the CLO. If the loan obtains credit approval, the investment team completes the last step of closing and funding the deal. The typical process from pre-screen to approval takes about two weeks for broadly syndicated loans. Closing and funding can take two or more weeks to complete after the approval date.

In the pre-screen, a credit analyst or other team member evaluates the information provided by the respective source and determines if the opportunity fits the investor's credit, structure, yield, and diversification parameters. If the analyst determines an opportunity is viable, he brings it to the investment committee for an initial screen.

The analyst will then provide the investment committee with a one- to two-page summary of the contemplated transaction that includes a checklist of screening criteria and briefly outlines the investment thesis, contemplated financing terms and structure, critical qualitative and quantitative points about the borrower, and potential risks subject to additional diligence. The investment committee will respond in one of three ways:

(1) Reject it since the key risks cannot be underwritten to its satisfaction.
(2) Approve to move forward but with several due diligence items identified as items that need to be addressed ("gating items").
(3) Recommend a strong mandate to pursue the opportunity and proceed expeditiously.

If an opportunity passes the initial investment committee screen, the analyst will assess likely leverage, pricing, and other transaction terms. Then, the analyst will provide the agent and/or sponsor/borrower with verbal indication of structure, pricing, and relevant terms (including but not limited to tenor, amortization, call provisions, financial maintenance, and other covenants and other transaction-specific terms).

The due diligence activities are guided by the gating items established during the initial screen discussion and receipt of all items on the standard diligence checklist. The due diligence process can include some of the following activities listed below.

- The investment team performs onsite company due diligence if possible.
- The analyst or team usually attends an in-person meeting or conference call organized by the agent and hosted by the management team and sponsor, who provide an overview of the transaction along with a Q&A session at the end. Broadly syndicated loan meetings or conference calls are usually split into public and private sections to accommodate the compliance requirements of the prospective lenders. The public-side lender group will forego seeing the projection model provided by the company's management team and will not be privy to other private information revealed in the private-side Q&A discussion. As most lenders take the management projections with a grain of salt, the absence of this data is not seen as a significant disadvantage for public lenders.
- Industry experts and consultants are engaged as needed to supplement onsite due diligence. Concerning expert calls, a call is held between the expert and the investment team after a suitable expert is found with the relevant company background and industry expertise. Picking the appropriate expert can be more challenging than it sounds. The expert can look great on paper, but once the call starts, the investment team can quickly ascertain that the expert does not have the relevant expertise needed to address the gating items. Spending extra time with the expert call advisor and vetting the experts before deciding which one to choose for the call is well worth the additional effort.

- Third-party accounting firms are engaged to perform a Quality of Earnings report and other financial analysis to the extent needed to validate financial reporting and cash flows.
- Legal counsel is engaged to assess legal risks and draft loan documentation.

In terms of ongoing dialogue, the investment team will go back and forth with the agent and/or management team/sponsor as the gating items are addressed, pricing and other terms are finalized, and additional questions arise. Sometimes the investment team will hold additional calls with the agent, sponsor and/or management team. These can be very helpful, especially when a lender meeting or call, as noted above, did not take place to officially introduce the transaction to the market. The investment team reports back to the investment committee periodically. If the dialogue or due diligence items prove to be unsatisfactory, the investment committee will decide to pass on the proposed transaction before a full investment committee meeting takes place, which frees up the investment team to pursue other opportunities.

When the investment team concludes that a transaction is in the interest of the fund to invest, the investment team formally recommends the investment to the investment committee. Prior to the meeting, the investment team distributes an investment memorandum, which is a complete set of materials that comprehensively describes the transaction, outlines key investment highlights and risks, details mitigating factors regarding gating items, includes due diligence results and feedback from expert calls and provides a summary of a full detailed financial model with base and stress case outcomes.

To the extent there are pre-close updates to financial results, final documentation, transaction structure, or pending confirmatory due diligence items, such updates are provided to the investment committee as received. If a transaction does not close within the expected timeframe, the investment team updates the investment committee as to the rationale for the delay.

Once the credit agreement and other legal documentation are finalized, the transaction closes, and funds. The investment team authorizes the trade, completes a trade ticket, and facilitates the wiring of funds to the agent bank. The bank will fund the loan first on its own balance sheet and then sell pieces of the loan to third parties shortly after close. This prevents any small loan investors from potentially not funding on time and holding up the process. The typical loan purchase (or sale) transaction usually settles seven days after the trade date but can take longer.

2.8 Borrower Projection Model

If the loan opportunity is going to be declined by the investment committee, the analysts may not bother receiving the private information. But if the transaction is likely, the investment team may receive a financial forecast, also referred to as the projection model, from the sponsor after the team has decided it's optimal to receive private information. As noted above, the optionality of whether to stay public or go private on a deal is quite common in the broadly syndicated loan market.

Private information generally includes projected financials (about a five-year forecast on average), which includes the income statement, balance sheet and statement of cash flows for each year, and a summary of the underlying assumptions that drive the forecast. Additional information could be provided, such as details regarding the ramp-up of a new business segment or a breakout of cost savings or synergies and the expected timing to achieve them. If the investment team remains public, they can still build a model quite easily from the historical financials along with some public guidance on a few items, such as the opening balance sheet, the company's tax rate, normal rate of capex spending, and typical working capital assumptions.

Regarding the sponsor model, it's usually an optimistic forecast and is taken with a grain of salt by the investment team. The sponsor usually forecasts revenue growth, margin expansion, and aggressive cost savings and/or synergies, resulting in the deal comfortably deleveraging from typically around 5x total leverage to 3x or 2x within several years. The analyst's job is to cut back the optimistic revenue growth assumptions, keep profit margins flat, and make a few other changes to capex or working capital to create a more realistic base-case scenario. The base case would also reduce many projected cost savings or synergies. In this case, leverage would trend sideways or perhaps step down a turn from 5x to 4x over a longer timeframe, such as four to five years. Liquidity would tighten from the sponsor case, but the company would generally still be able to comfortably meet its fixed charges, such as interest expense, principal amortization, and taxes.

The analyst's next step is to sensitize the model even further and run a more draconian downside case. In this scenario, the analyst most likely builds in a recession with several years of material revenue declines, brings down profit margins to at least the lowest level they've been historically, and makes a few other tweaks to hit the financials negatively. In this case, leverage could increase quite rapidly from 5x to about the 8x or 9x range within two or three years, and liquidity would worsen to the point where the company may not have the cash to meet interest and principal payments and would have to draw on the revolving line of credit.

Developing the downside case scenario is more of an art than a science. The point is to see how big a negative hit a prospective borrower can take before the company cannot service its debt.

A downside case scenario can consider future recessions, loss of a large customer, margin erosion due to changes in product pricing or raw material cost dynamics, higher than expected capex, and many other factors.

The point with the financial modeling is that the lenders do not benefit from the upside if the business performs well. They're hyper focused on outcomes where the loan is not repaid at par.

2.9 Leveraged Loan Monitoring

Once the credit approval process has run its course and the loan purchase has been completed, the loan becomes a holding in the CLO's portfolio, and the investment team is now responsible for monitoring it. The monitoring process generally follows a quarterly cadence since that is the typical timing for reporting a company's financial results. Each quarter, a company is required to post its financial results within a specified number of days after the quarter-end. Usually, the required reporting date is 45 days after quarter end, but it can be up to 60 or even 75 days, especially for the first few quarters after closing a new acquisition.

These financial reporting requirements are typically stipulated in the Credit Agreement in Section 6, Affirmative Covenants. Most companies report on a calendar-year basis, so quarterly results would normally be posted to lenders on May 15, August 15, and November 15. Credit analysts can expect to be busy reviewing financial results at these times of the year. For year-end results, which include the annual audit and fourth-quarter results, the reporting period is longer, typically 90 days up to 120 days. Therefore, there can be a lengthy reporting "black hole" where the borrower provides no new information between the September 30 quarterly results, due on November 15, and the annual/fourth quarter December 31 results, due on or about March 30. The annual reporting package generally includes the audit. Borrowers quite often post preliminary fourth-quarter and full-year results before March 30, which can be very helpful. For new transactions involving a merger, the first audit is quite often delayed as the auditors need more time to finalize the combined financials of both the acquirer and target. The lenders then grant a one-time waiver, and the audit is allowed to be delivered later, usually within 30 or 60 days.

The following deliverables are expected to be received by the investment team from each borrower:

- Quarterly financial results compared to the prior year and budget if specified in the Credit Agreement.
- Quarterly Compliance Certificate signed by an officer, usually the CFO.
- Quarterly compliance calculation document sets forth the underlying compliance calculations used to determine the leverage ratio, interest coverage ratio, and any other metric required for compliance purposes.
- Quarterly Management Discussion and Analysis (MD&A) if required by the Credit Agreement.
- Quarterly call with management if required by the Credit Agreement.
- Annual budget, which is typically required 60 or 90 days after year-end.
- Annual audit.
- Loans in technical default may require monthly reporting per a negotiated forbearance agreement with the lenders. In that case, a common deliverable is a monthly liquidity report in the form of a 13-week cash flow forecast created by a third-party financial consultant hired by the lenders and paid for by the company.

Each loan in the CLO is usually assigned an initial rating by the investment team or investment committee. After the credit analyst has reviewed the quarterly results and prepared a summary report, the investment team will opine on any appropriate changes to the internal ratings assigned to each investment in the portfolio. The investment team will decide to either affirm the existing rating or recommend a downgrade or upgrade. At a quarterly review meeting, the investment committee will make the final decision and approve the rating it deems suitable. The internal rating does not play a role in any of the CLO's many tests. A sample list of internal ratings and respective criteria is provided below.

- Grade A loans represent the least amount of credit risk in the portfolio. The borrower is performing above expectations, with favorable trends and risk factors.
- Grade B loans have an acceptable risk level similar to the risk at the time of origination. The borrower generally performs as expected, and risk factors are neutral to favorable.
- Grade C loans are performing below expectations, and risk has increased somewhat since origination, but the borrower is current on its interest and principal.
- Grade D loans are typically in technical default and may be in payment default. The borrower is performing materially below expectations, and risk has increased materially since origination.
- Grade E loans are expected to be worked out in a restructuring process where the lender does not receive its full interest and principal.

Most investment teams will develop a watch list of the loans in technical default or worse. In the sample list above, Grade D and E loans would be added to a watch list for increased monitoring. The investment team would provide regular updates to the investment committee on these credits. These updates would summarize current operating results, material impending events, proposed solutions, and actions taken by co-lenders and other stakeholders (including but not limited to amendments, forbearance/waivers, and restructuring support agreements). The investment team would recommend how to best preserve value and enhance recoveries for these loans.

Some investment teams develop a risk matrix that combines the internal credit ratings of the loans with another metric or financial figure, such as the leverage ratio, and use the resulting grid to determine the maximum dollar size of the investment, usually expressed as a loan's percentage of the total portfolio. The internal credit ratings could be on the X axis, the leverage ratio on the Y axis, and the recommended loan size in the resulting boxes of the grid.

2.10 Historical Loan Defaults and Recoveries

The private equity firm that acquires a business may be targeting returns of 20% or higher. But there is a significant risk to achieving those returns. The owner of a leveraged loan is targeting high-single-digit returns but taking much less risk. If the business has multiple quarters of poor earnings, usually, the leveraged loan will eventually be repaid at par. Moderate deterioration in the enterprise value of a business is solely a problem for the private equity owners. However, if underperformance is severe, a default may arise. Historically, the default rate for broadly syndicated loans is below 2% in times when the economy is growing, but in recessionary times like the GFC, the rate increased to the 8% range. Some factors that may push a business into default are (1) loss of large customers, (2) technological change, (3) regulatory change, and (4) new competition.

Leveraged Loan Default Rate

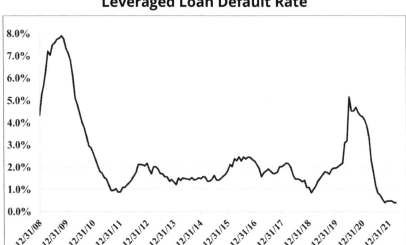

Source: JP Morgan Research

In CLOs specifically, there had been an uptick in defaults from March 2022 to March 2023, but the overall rate was still quite low. CLOs will generally invest in leveraged loans with lower default rates than the overall Loan Index.

Recent Default Rates for Leveraged Loans in CLOs

CLO Vintage	Mar-23	Mar-22	Change
2013	1.08%	0.61%	0.47%
2014	1.05%	0.33%	0.72%
2015	0.87%	0.36%	0.51%
2016	0.98%	0.38%	0.60%
2017	1.01%	0.17%	0.84%
2018	0.81%	0.20%	0.61%
2019	0.65%	0.09%	0.57%
2020	0.38%	0.00%	0.38%
2021	0.14%	0.00%	0.14%
2022	0.00%	0.00%	0.00%
All	0.51%	0.10%	0.41%

Source: Moody's Investor Service

For an investor in leveraged loans, the loan loss rate—not the default rate—is the important driver of returns. The loss on the leveraged loan is determined by the recovery rate in the event of a default. Some leveraged loans have defaulted and recovered 100% of their par balance, resulting in no loss of principal for the lender. Other leveraged loans have experienced dismal recoveries, like some oil and gas companies, when commodity prices fell dramatically in 2015/2016.

The first lien loan is the first in line for payment in bankruptcy, with a lien on all the company's assets. And the initial equity in the business, contributed by a private equity firm, takes the first loss.

Historical Recoveries

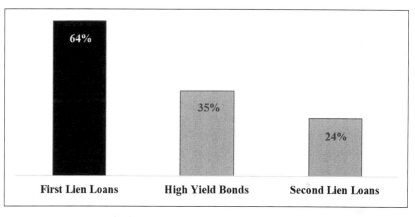

Source: JP Morgan Default Monitor December 2022. The first lien loan recovery is for the period January 1, 1990, to December 31, 2022. High yield bonds recovery rate is for the period January 1, 1982, to December 31, 2022. Second lien loan recovery rate is for the period January 1, 2008, to December 31, 2022.

While the averages are shown above, it's important to note that the recovery rate can be volatile. In recessionary periods, recovery rates decrease as more businesses default into poor economic conditions. In 2022, the average recovery rate was 53%, well below historical averages. However, the default rate in 2022 was also low by historical standards, at less than 1.0%.

The recovery rates above are measured by the trading price of the leveraged loan 30 days after the company defaults. However, most CLOs can hold the leveraged loan through the bankruptcy process and would expect a higher recovery after the restructuring is complete. Often, the CLO managers sell leveraged loans at a higher price before default.

When the recovery rate is instead calculated by ultimate recovery, Fitch Ratings cites a 76% average first lien recovery rate from 2002 to 2021.

NON-RATING ACTION COMMENTARY

First-Lien Term Loan Recoveries Dip in 2020, Begin to Recover in 2021

Mon 21 March, 2022 - 3:18 PM ET

Related Fitch Ratings Content: U.S. Leveraged Finance Restructuring Series: Ultimate Recovery Rate Study (First-Lien Term Loan Recoveries Dip in 2020, Begin to Recover in 2021)

Fitch Ratings-New York-21 March 2022: A decrease in first-lien term loan recoveries, driven by the pandemic, has begun to reverse, with 2021 ultimate recoveries reverting back to historical levels, according to a new Fitch Ratings report.

"The coronavirus pandemic, resulting EBITDA pressures and a trend toward encumbering an increasing share of enterprise or asset value with first-lien debt, prior to filing, helped drive down recoveries in 2020," said Judah Gross, Senior Director at Fitch.

The average recovery rate in 2020 was 67 percent, and the median was 80 percent. Valuations were heavily pressured by the pandemic-induced market volatility, uncertainty and recession. Forty-three percent of claims were in the energy; retail; gaming, lodging and restaurant; or leisure sectors, all of which faced significant stress in 2020. Average first-lien term loan recoveries for these sectors were materially below the 2020 and overall dataset averages.

An 85 percent average ultimate recovery for the 2021 filers suggests a return to historical levels as U.S. corporate distress subsided last year. Several 2021 filers still subject to the bankruptcy process, with first-lien term loans not yet included in our dataset, are expected to see recoveries in the 91–100 percent range. The 2021 sample size is limited given that bankruptcy filing volume has also dwindled in 2021.

Historically, first-lien term loan recoveries have been strong with 52 percent of claims obtaining ultimate recoveries of 91–100 percent. The average recovery rate is 76 percent, and the median is 96 percent across all first-lien term loans in Fitch's bankruptcy case study dataset spanning 2002-2021.

Recoveries on second-lien debt claims were only marginally higher than unsecured notes. The average second-lien ultimate recovery was 39 percent and 38 percent of the cohort recovered 10 percent or less. There was a similarly wide dispersion around the 35 percent average unsecured note recovery. Roughly 42 percent of unsecured note claims recovered 10 percent or less, but 22 percent recovered 71 percent or more of the claim amount.

Source: Fitch Ratings

2.11 Historical Loan Returns

The Morningstar LSTA Leveraged Loan Index (the "Loan Index") tracks the performance of the broadly syndicated loan market. Usually, the index trades close to par value, but there are always some borrowers whose leveraged loans trade at discounted levels that pull the overall index down. Leveraged Loans can occasionally trade above par value for short periods, but in those markets, the leveraged loans tend to be refinanced with new loans at lower spreads. Ultimately, par is the best final payment a leveraged loan offers unless there is a prepayment penalty early in the leveraged loan's life.

Since 2000, the average Loan Index annual return has been 5.3%. The performance of leveraged loans as an asset class is critical to the CLO structure. It's why a CLO's most senior notes can be rated AAA, on par with bonds issued by the US Government. It's also why a $500 million CLO only needs $50 million of equity, while the remainder can be borrowed.

CLOs use leverage and structure to turn leveraged loan returns into the potential for double-digit returns for the owners of CLO equity. The favorable returns also speak to the quality of the collateral that backs the CLO BB Note.

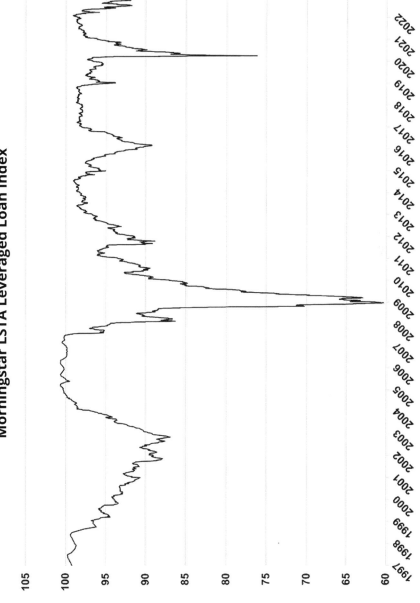

Morningstar LSTA Leveraged Loan Index

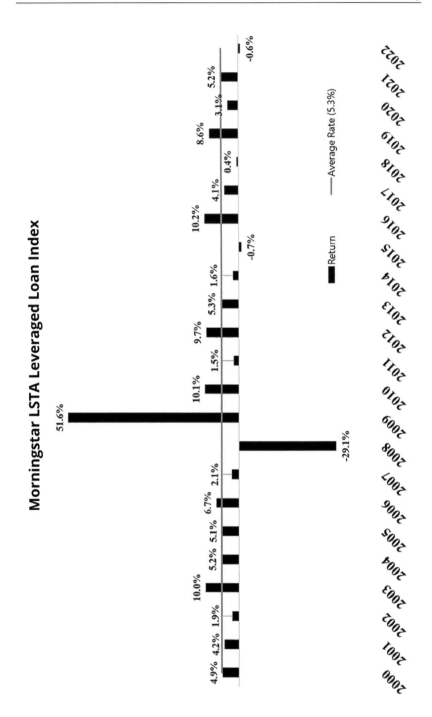

Morningstar LSTA Leveraged Loan Index

2000: 4.9%
2001: 4.2%
2002: 1.9%
2003: 10.0%
2004: 5.2%
2005: 5.1%
2006: 6.7%
2007: 2.1%
2008: -29.1%
2009: 51.6%
2010: 10.1%
2011: 1.5%
2012: 9.7%
2013: 5.3%
2014: 1.6%
2015: -0.7%
2016: 10.2%
2017: 4.1%
2018: 0.4%
2019: 8.6%
2020: 3.1%
2021: 5.2%
2022: -0.6%

Return
Average Rate (5.3%)

The Loan Index had positive returns for all but three of the last 20 years.

The Loan Index fell sharply in 2008 as the financial crisis negatively impacted leveraged loans, and it seemed possible the entire banking system could fail. At that time, many of the owners of leveraged loans had financed their purchases with mark-to-market financing lines called Total Return Swaps. As the leveraged loans began to decline in value, the owners of the leveraged loans were forced to sell to meet margin calls. Forced selling in an environment with few leveraged loan buyers resulted in increased downward pressure on leveraged loan prices and even more forced selling. It was a vicious cycle. The loan market bounced back sharply in 2009 as the technical backdrop for loans improved. The Total Return Swap structure is no longer widely used because of this negative experience.

Another negative return year for the Loan Index was 2015. As commodity prices fell at the end of that year, ~5% of loans tied to commodity prices began trading at distressed levels.

During the spring of 2020, the COVID-19 pandemic sent the loan market tumbling from 97 to 76 cents on the dollar. However, loans still rose 3% for the year, as expectations for leveraged loan defaults abated quickly during the year.

In 2022 the Loan Index returned −0.6%, as the increased risk of recession weighed on the market. Compared to other asset classes, leveraged loans materially outperformed. The chart below highlights the value of being floating rate and first lien during economic headwinds.

Asset Class Returns 2022

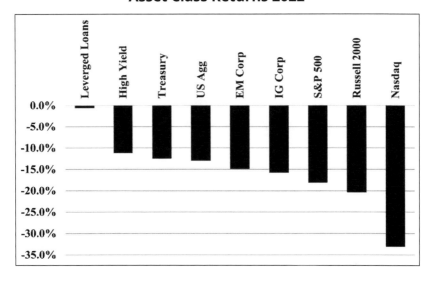

CLO Participants

3.1 CLO Manager

The CLO's collateral manager picks the initial loans for the CLO and keeps it fully invested through the reinvestment period. Additionally, the collateral manager will ensure that the CLO passes its many compliance tests. CLO managers usually charge a fee of between 30 bps and 50 bps annually on total assets to perform this function. Additionally, there is typically an incentive fee of 20.0% of equity cash flows after realized returns exceed a 12.0% hurdle.

For the CLO's equity and BB investor, adequate diligence of the CLO manager is paramount, given the manager's role in investment selection and portfolio construction. It's important to find CLO managers that have superior access to leveraged loans and an experienced investment team. However, if the CLO exits its reinvestment period, the CLO manager's role is significantly reduced.

The CLO manager will typically be incentivized to buy leveraged loans that have high spreads to maximize interest income into the CLO. But high spreads are also associated with more leveraged loan default risk. Indeed, the leveraged loan market is rather efficient. Because the CLO is 10x leveraged, the CLO manager's role is to play it safe with its investment decisions and let the CLO's leverage generate the equity returns. "Shooting layups" is an analogy to describe this investment style. Generally, a CLO manager wouldn't buy distressed loans into the CLO other than potentially swapping one distressed loan already owned for another with better recovery prospects.

One way that CLO managers differentiate themselves is their willingness to invest in leveraged loans with less than $500 million outstanding. These smaller syndicated loans will have less secondary market liquidity but will also come with a higher spread.

Below is a checklist to evaluate a CLO manager. However, each criterion is incomplete or deficient in some way. The result is that choosing CLO managers is more of an art than a science.

Criteria	Pros	Cons
Manager Default and Recovery Stats	Key determinant of CLO equity's returns	Doesn't factor in loan spread differentials among managers, i.e. higher spread compensates for larger loan losses
		Managers can sell loans at discounts prior to default to have a lower default %
		The Manager's inception date can play a big factor
		Doesn't factor in discounted loans bought that may ultimately recover par
Changes in Amount of Par Values of Loans	Building par value implies higher equity returns	Managers can buy discounted loans that increase the par balance, so the outcome depends on if the loans are ultimately repaid at par
		Doesn't factor in the riskiness of the underlying par value of the loans
Amount of CCC/Caa-Rated Loans Owned	Low loan ratings can be a precursor to default	CCC/Caa loans may not default
		The manager may have proactively bought CCC/Caa loans to increse portfolio spread
		Most investors value the credit analysis of the Manager over the assesment of the rating agency
Amount of Loans Trading Below 80 or 90	Discounted loans are precursor to default	Discounted loans may not default
		Manager may have proactively bought discounted loans
		Discounted loans can be the result of low spread, not just credit risk

Criteria	Pros	Cons
Quarterly Distributions	Higher distributions should lead to higher equity IRR	Doesn't factor in a NAV that could be declining
		Can be influenced by the amount of leverage the CLO uses
		Highly dependent on the vintage that prior CLOs were issued in
		Doesn't consider the riskiness of the underlying loans
CLO NAV	Higher NAV implies better CLO performance	Doesn't factor in equity distributions
		If loans are trading above par, NAV will be inflated, and loans are ultimately repaid at par
CLO Cost of Debt	Lower cost of debt implies better equity cash flows	Debt investors may prefer CLO managers that run very diversified portfolios that simply mimic the Loan Index
		Debt investors may prefer managers with brand names over managers with better equity returns
Active CLO Management	Preference for managers actively optimizing the portfolio	Active loan trading, in itself, does not add value

A separate qualitative way to evaluate managers is to consider who is doing the actual work on the loan investments. These are generally not the people in the room during most CLO due diligence meetings. Is it someone learning about the business model for the first time? Or someone with years of industry experience supported by firm-wide resources? Below is a simplified diagram that illustrates the depth of a CLO manager's investment team.

Credit Analysis Completed by	
Generalist who covers many industries	
Generalist who uses outside expert networks	Value Added
Team of credit analysts that cover one industry only	
Analyst team benefits from credit insights from the firm's teams in distressed loans / private equity	
Analyst team benefits from credit insights from the firm's private equity team that bidded for the company	

While picking "good" leveraged loans is the primary role of the CLO manager, a secondary function is optimizing the CLO's distributions and tests. The CLO's rules are complex, and a good CLO manager knows how to extract the most value from the CLO for its equity investors.

CLO managers are often described as equity-friendly or debt-friendly. An equity-friendly manager might run a higher-spread portfolio, buy more leveraged loans with lower ratings and do everything possible to keep the CLO fully invested after the reinvestment period. A debt-friendly manager considers the interests of the CLO's noteholders and generally manages more conservatively.

Many CLO equity investors will focus on CLO managers that assemble lower-spread pools of leveraged loans. The reason is that these leveraged loans are believed to have lower default risk. Also, Japanese CLO investors, especially for Notes AAA to A, often offer the lowest debt costs for the CLO, and lower spread portfolios are important to attract these investors. This is important for the initial CLO as well as potential refinancings or resets in the future.

Many of the largest US asset managers are also the largest CLO managers. A ranking from Creditflux, the paper of record for the CLO industry, is shown below. Blackstone, Palmer Square, and Elmwood lead the rankings, but there are over 120 active CLO managers to choose from.

Top 10 CLO Managers — 2022

Rank	Manager	Size ($bn)	Market Share
1	Blackstone	6.8	5.7%
2	Palmer Square	5.6	4.7%
3	Elmwood	4.5	3.8%
4	PGIM	4.4	3.7%
5	Octagon	3.6	3.0%
6	KKR	3.5	3.0%
7	Neuberger Berman	3.4	2.9%
8	Ares	3.4	2.9%
9	CIFC	3.3	2.8%
10	CSAM	3.1	2.6%

Source: Creditflux

CLO market participants like to divide managers into different tiers. For example, a CLO manager that has a large investor following is considered tier one, while a newer CLO manager might be tier three. A CLO manager that has underperformed on the leveraged loans might be regarded as tier four. While a few CLO managers clearly reside in tier one, the rest of the managers' tiers are debatable. This is because different CLO investors will put different weights on the factors in the CLO manager checklist above.

A CLO manager that can obtain low-cost debt financing on its CLO Notes is certainly a good argument for a tier-one categorization. As the cost of debt on different CLO Notes is public information, it's clear who those managers are.

The CLO market has no shortage of data to analyze about a manager's performance. But there is a qualitative aspect to choosing CLO managers as well. Many CLO investors develop favorable working relationships with certain CLO managers and prefer to work with those managers on future CLOs. The industry views it as a positive sign if a CLO manager meets frequently with his or her investors to discuss the CLO's performance. Trust and relationships are vital in a market where each CLO is bespoke.

There are four ways the CLO manager and the CLO equity investor are aligned:

- The incentive fee is achieved only when a realized return above 12% has been generated for the CLO equity. This is a high but attainable hurdle to hit.
- Reputation is crucial to the manager. If the CLO manager underperforms on one of its deals, it will be harder for the CLO manager to win mandates for subsequent CLOs.
- Though not required to do so, many CLO managers will also invest in the CLO equity of their deals.
- Occasionally the CLO manager will subsidize the CLO equity owned by a third-party investor. That could be done by arranging for the CLO equity to be bought for a more favorable price than that paid by the CLO manager. This construct may work for the manager as it will also benefit from the fees associated with managing the CLO.

There are also circumstances when the manager and the CLO equity investor may not be aligned:

- The CLO manager may be incentivized to keep the CLO outstanding longer than the CLO equity investor thinks is optimal, as the CLO management fee stream will terminate when the CLO is liquidated. However, a majority of the CLO's equity can decide when to call the deal.

- When a CLO manager issues CLOs after the one you have participated in, they need to show potential new CLO Note investors that the existing CLOs don't have too many defaulted or CCC/Caa-rated leveraged loans. That could mean selling some stressed leveraged loans from your CLO at prices that the manager might not otherwise accept to aid in issuing future deals you aren't involved in.

- A CLO manager can only be in the market with one new issue CLO and one refinancing simultaneously. If the manager has multiple CLOs eligible for refinancing, the manager often chooses the CLO that has been out of the non-call period the longest. But they aren't required to do so.

If you have the pleasure of meeting with many CLO managers, you may find they are a relatively undifferentiated group. They usually all have decent-sized teams of credit analysts, senior leaders with extensive experience in the market, and resources to deal with poor-performing leveraged loans. By nature, it's a conservative group. When you find one that has outperformed, you may wonder, "what is the secret sauce?" And what is the likelihood it will continue outperforming its peers? The answers are hard to identify. Leveraged loan defaults are rare, and missing a few key ones could lead to material outperformance. Luck certainly plays a role. With most CLO managers, employees have moved from one firm to another so that any proprietary processes would have been shared across firms long ago. Some years were better than others for launching a CLO management platform, and the vintage bias may persist over time.

One area where outperformance is perpetuated is in the CLO Note interest rates. Firms with good track records that frequently issue CLOs generally receive more attractive CLO Note costs from the perspective of the equity. These lower debt costs can be material for the CLO equity investor, given the leverage in the

CLO. Sometimes lower CLO Note costs are simply awarded for being a manager with a well-known brand name. In some cases, the lower debt costs are offset by higher CLO management fees.

3.2 CLO Arranger

A CLO arranger is the investment bank that brings a CLO to life. Its role is to place all the CLO's Notes with market participants. It mediates all negotiations between the various investors in the CLO but usually doesn't invest in the CLO. The arranger receives a one-time fee of approximately 20 to 40 bps of the CLO's total liabilities as compensation.

The leading CLO arrangers are some of the world's largest investment banks.

CLO Arranger Rankings — 2022

Rank	Arranger	Size ($bn)	Market Share
1	BofA	17.4	14.7%
2	Citi	16.2	13.7%
3	JP Morgan	13.7	11.6%
4	Barclays	11.3	9.5%
5	Morgan Stanley	10.2	8.6%
6	Goldman Sachs	9.1	7.7%
7	Credit Suisse	7.4	6.3%
8	Jefferies	5.8	4.7%
9	BNP Paribas	5.5	4.6%
10	Natixis	3.9	3.3%

Source: Creditflux

It takes a considerable amount of work to bring a CLO into existence. The investors in the different CLO securities have wildly competing agendas. For example, the AAA Note wants as many constraints on the CLO's leveraged loans as possible, while the equity tranche wants the least. Additionally, the CLO manager, lawyers, and rating agencies must all agree on the terms in the CLO's indenture. It's only because precedents have been set for what the CLO's multiple parties should expect that CLOs can be formed so frequently.

The fee to the CLO arranger is a negotiated item. If the formation of the CLO goes smoothly, the CLO arranger may make an elevated fee. If the equity is not easy to sell, the CLO arranger may reduce its fee to increase the equity returns.

There are several ways CLO arrangers differentiate themselves:

- Access to CLO leveraged loans. If a CLO arranger has an active pipeline of broadly syndicated loan opportunities, that arranger may be chosen if preferential allocations of the leveraged loans can go into the new CLO.
- Warehouse terms. Prior to forming a CLO, a warehousing financing line is usually started to CLO acquire leveraged loans. Terms can vary, and some arrangers will offer favorable terms as an enticement to select them as arranger.
- Expertise and deal flow. The busier CLO arrangers are in constant contact with market participants and may obtain better CLO execution as a result.
- Willingness to take on tougher mandates. Some of the smaller CLO arrangers may be willing to work on CLOs for emerging managers, where the market needs to be educated on the CLO manager's platform capabilities.

3.3 Rating Agencies

Rating agencies have two important roles in the CLO ecosystem. First, they rate the CLO's leveraged loans. The rating is usually established when the leveraged loan is first created, and the rating agency publishes a multi-page report with its analysis. The most common rating agencies in the CLO ecosystem are Moody's, S&P, and Fitch. Their ratings are an independent third-party assessment of a borrower's credit quality. The ratings they assign using the S&P ratings scale goes from AAA to D. For leveraged loans, the relevant ratings will be BB and below.

Rating	Grade	Definition
AAA	Investment	Extremely strong capacity to meet financial commitments
AA	Investment	Very strong capacity to meet financial commitments
A	Investment	Strong capacity to meet financial commitments, but somewhat susceptible to economic conditions and changes in circumstances
BBB	Investment	Adequate capacity to meet financial commitments, but more subject to adverse economic conditions
BB	Speculative	Less vulnerable in the near-term but faces major ongoing uncertainties to adverse business, financial, and economic conditions
B	Speculative	More vulnerable to adverse business, financial and economic conditions but currently has the capacity to meet financial commitments
CCC	Speculative	Currently vulnerable and dependent on favorable business, financial and economic conditions to meet financial commitments
CC	Speculative	Highly vulnerable; default has not yet occurred, but is expected to be a virtual certainty
C	Speculative	Currently highly vulnerable to non-payment, and ultimate recovery is expected to be lower than that of higher rated obligations
D	Speculative	Payment default on a financial commitment or breach of an imputed promise; also used when a bankruptcy petition has been filed

Source: S&P Global Ratings

Each letter rating is tied to a statistical probability that a loan will default over a given time period. To derive their ratings, the agencies have models that use similar factors to the credit analysis in Section 2.2 above.

The qualitative rating categories above are linked to statistical probabilities of default. For example, a loan initially rated B, the most common rating for a leveraged loan in a CLO, has a 12.2% probability of default by the end of year three. A leveraged loan initially rated BB would have a 4.1% default probability over the same time.

Average Cumulative Default Rates For Corporates By Region (1981-2021)										
	Time Horizon (Years)									
Rating	1	2	3	4	5	6	7	8	9	10
BB	0.7%	2.2%	4.1%	5.8%	7.4%	9.0%	10.3%	11.6%	12.7%	13.7%
B	3.4%	8.0%	12.2%	15.5%	18.1%	20.3%	22.0%	23.3%	24.5%	25.7%
CCC/C	28.3%	40.0%	45.7%	49.3%	51.8%	53.0%	54.3%	55.1%	55.9%	56.5%

Source: S&P Global Ratings

In a newly issued leveraged loan, the private equity firm purchasing a company will usually want to employ as much leverage as possible. However, the prospective buyers of the leveraged loan will need a minimum rating to buy it into the CLO. For example, a newly issued leveraged loan rated CCC would probably not work for many CLOs. Leveraged loans with BB ratings often work well for a CLO because they increase the overall ratings of the CLO's portfolio and help with the CLO's mandatory compliance tests. However, BB-rated leveraged loans would also have a lower spread.

Below is an excerpt from a ratings report for a common holding in CLOs. A report like this is generated when the leveraged loan is initially formed or when a material refinancing occurs. A leveraged loan will need a rating before it can be added to the CLO.

Fitch Affirms Charter's 'BB+' Ratings; Rates Unsecured Notes 'BB+'/'RR4'; Outlook Stable

Thu 04 Aug, 2022 - 4:03 PM ET

Fitch Ratings - New York - 04 Aug 2022: Fitch Ratings has affirmed the 'BB+' Issuer Default Ratings (IDRs) of Charter Communications Operating, LLC (CCO), CCO Holdings, LLC (CCOH), Time Warner Cable, LLC (TWC) and Time Warner Cable Enterprises LLC (TWCE) and assigned a 'BB+' Long-Term IDR to Charter Communications, Inc. (Charter). Fitch has also affirmed the 'BBB-'/'RR1' senior secured ratings for instruments at CCO, TWC, and TWCE and the 'BB+'/'RR4' senior unsecured ratings for instruments at CCOH. The Rating Outlook is Stable.

Fitch has also assigned a 'BB+'/'RR4' rating to CCOH's proposed benchmark issuance. Charter is expected to use net proceeds for general corporate purposes, including potential buybacks of class A common stock of Charter or common units of Charter Communications Holdings, LLC (CCH), a subsidiary of Charter, repayment of indebtedness, and to pay related fees and expenses. As of June 30, 2022, Charter's stock buyback program had the authority to purchase an additional $673 million of its class A common stock and CCH common units.

Fitch has also assigned a 'BBB-'/'RR1' rating to CCO's Term Loans A-5 and A-6, the net proceeds of which were used for repayment of existing indebtedness.

Fitch has withdrawn the 'BBB-'/'RR1' ratings on Charter's Term Loan A-4 as they were repaid in full in May 2022.

KEY RATING DRIVERS

Leading Market Position: Charter is the second-largest U.S. cable MVPD behind Comcast Corp. Charter's 32.1 million customer relationships at June 30, 2022 provide significant scale benefits.

Credit Profile: Revenue and EBITDA in the LTM ended June 30, 2022 totaled $53.2 billion and $21.4 billion, respectively. As of June 30, 2022, Charter had approximately $95.7 billion of debt outstanding, including $70.6 billion of senior secured debt. Fitch estimates total Fitch-calculated gross leverage was 4.5x while secured leverage was 3.3x for LTM ended June 30, 2022, well within Fitch's negative rating sensitivities.

Continued Operating Momentum: Charter's operating strategies are strengthening its competitive position and operating metrics while expanding margins. The company is focusing on a market share-driven strategy, leveraging its all-digital infrastructure to enhance its service offerings' overall competitiveness. As a result, revenues increased to $53.2 billion for the LTM ended June 30, 2022 from $41.6 billion in 2017 while Fitch-calculated margins improved by 340 bps to 40.2%, as Charter's wireless business moves toward break-even and the cable business continues its positive operating momentum.

Product Mix Shift: Internet services (broadband) revenue surpassed video services revenue in 2020 and became the company's largest segment as consumers became increasingly reliant on broadband's capabilities during the pandemic, including facilitating access to video streaming services and working from home.

Fitch continues to believe broadband growth will offset the expected continued industrywide decline in basic video subscribers while also benefiting margins and FCF, given broadband's higher margins and lower capital intensity. Wireless is expected to see continued growth and eventually offset related infrastructure spending, however systemwide rollout costs are expected to continue to be a drag on near-term total margins.

Broadband Growth: Fitch expects broadband additions will continue to slow over the rating horizon as Charter approaches penetration saturation in its existing footprint, coupled with the pressure of the significant pull forward of broadband additions as a result of the pandemic. Fitch expects ARPU growth to drive broadband revenue growth in the low- to mid-single digits over the rating horizon. Charter plans to continue to expand its footprint, which has grown to 55 million homes and businesses passed at June 30, 2022 from 50.3 million at YE 2017. For 2022, Charter guided total capex of $7.1 billion to $7.3 billion excluding capex associated with its mobile and rural construction initiative.

Charter expects to spend $5 billion over the next six years on a rural construction initiative build out broadband capabilities in unserved areas ($589 million spent in 1H22).

To help fund this, Charter will receive an aggregate $1.2 billion over 10 years from the Rural Digital Opportunity Fund (RDOF). Although the aggregate footprint expansion provides growth potential, Fitch is unsure penetration levels will replicate historical levels, especially in currently unserved areas.

Wireless Offering: Fitch believes Charter's wireless service expansion offers further operating leverage improvement through scaling benefits. In November 2020, Charter extended and expanded its mobile virtual network operator (MVNO) agreement with Verizon Communications Inc. To bolster network capabilities and connectivity and further reduce its dependency on the MVNO, Charter has been building out and deploying the Citizen Broadband Radio Service spectrum it purchased in 2020. Each of these actions is expected to drive margin improvements.

Source: Fitch Ratings

After that, the company's initial ratings are given, performance is monitored, and the rating can be adjusted up or down. An increase in financial leverage would be a reason for a ratings downgrade, while deleveraging would be a rationale for an upgrade.

Ratings History for a Defaulted Issuer

Isagenix Worldwide Inc. Downgraded To 'D' From 'CCC' On Forbearance Agreement, Missed Payments

U.S.-based multilevel marketer Isagenix Worldwide Inc. entered into a forbearance agreement with term loan and revolving credit facility lenders in anticipation of missing third-quarter principal and interest payments. The agreement provides relief until Nov. 15, 2022.

As a result of the agreement and our understanding that principal and interest payments due Sept. 30, 2022, will be missed, we lowered our issuer credit rating on Isagenix to 'D' from 'CCC'.

We also affirmed the 'D' issue-level rating on the company's term loan and lowered the rating on the revolving credit facility to 'D' from 'B-'. We lowered the recovery rating on senior secured debt claims to '3', reflecting our expectation for meaningful recovery (50%-70%; rounded estimate: 65%) in the event of a payment default.

CHICAGO (S&P Global Ratings) Sept. 30, 2022—S&P Global Ratings today took the rating actions listed above.

The downgrade reflects Isagenix's decision to seek forbearance on principal and interest payments on its term loan and revolving credit facility ahead of the Sept. 30 due date. Under the agreement dated Sept. 23, the term loan and revolving credit facility lenders agreed to not exercise or enforce certain remedies related to this nonpayment until Nov. 15. In our view, this represents a default on the term loan and revolving credit facility because Isagenix is distressed, it will not meet its contractual obligation to pay principal and interest in a timely manner, and it did not adequately compensate lenders for agreeing to

> temporarily waive their rights. We understand that the company's decision to seek forbearance and miss the payments was driven by a severe decline in operating performance due to instability of its multilevel marketing business model, resulting in weak cash flow and tightened liquidity. As of Sept. 28, Isagenix had fully drawn its $30 million revolver and had $14 million cash on hand.
>
> We will reevaluate our rating on the company when a debt restructuring is announced.

Source: S&P Global Ratings

Overall upgrade and downgrade ratios give investors in CLOs a sense of the underlying performance of the CLO's leveraged loans. An excess of downgrades to CCC/Caa is a risk for CLO equity and CLO BB Note investors because of the potential to have their cash flows diverted.

Rating agencies' second role is to rate the CLO's Notes. The agencies have statistical models that use the underlying ratings of the CLO's leveraged loans to determine the probability of default for each of the CLO's Notes. That probability is then tied back to a rating. The rating agencies publish many details for how their CLO ratings are determined. The framework often includes a Monte Carlo simulator that runs thousands of potential leveraged loan loss scenarios. As shown below, according to Moody's, a CLO BB Note's cumulative 10-year probability of default is 3.9% or 0.39% annually.

Global CLOs, Multiyear Withdraw(WR)-Unadjusted Cumulative Impairment Rates By Original Rating, 1993-2021											
		Horizon Year									
Rating	CLOs Rated	1	2	3	4	5	6	7	8	9	10
AAA	5,070	0.0%	0.0%	0.0%	0.0%	0.0%	0.0%	0.0%	0.0%	0.0%	0.0%
AA	2,609	0.0%	0.0%	0.0%	0.0%	0.0%	0.0%	0.0%	0.0%	0.0%	0.0%
A	2,344	0.0%	0.0%	0.1%	0.1%	0.1%	0.1%	0.1%	0.1%	0.1%	0.1%
BAA	2,236	0.0%	0.0%	0.1%	0.2%	0.5%	0.5%	0.8%	1.5%	1.7%	1.7%
BA	1,937	0.0%	0.1%	0.3%	0.5%	0.8%	1.6%	1.9%	2.7%	3.2%	3.9%
B	408	0.0%	0.3%	1.1%	1.1%	2.7%	8.6%	9.1%	9.1%	9.1%	9.1%

Source: Moody's Investor Service

Like leveraged loan ratings, the rating agencies monitor the CLO Note ratings and change them as warranted by the CLO's performance.

During the COVID-19 downturn, many CLO Notes were put on review for possible downgrade, but it seems the alarm was unwarranted.

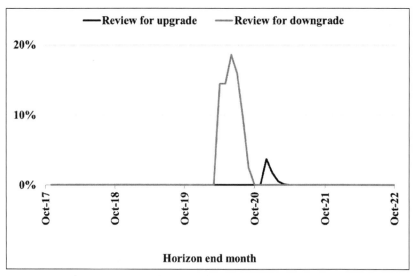

Source: Moody's Investor Service

Choosing the rating agency(ies) for the CLOs Notes is usually a decision that is not of primary concern for the CLO equity investor. The CLO's equity is not rated because it does not offer any contractual return—it only receives the excess cash flow each quarter. Indeed, since some leveraged loans are expected to default, it's unlikely the CLO's equity tranche would get back to par when the CLO is liquidated.

Usually, the CLO equity investor wants to minimize his equity commitment to the CLO. He may find that one rating agency may permit slightly higher leverage than another while still obtaining the ratings required by the CLO's Note investors. At the AAA level, an investor may require ratings from two rating agencies, so the CLO must be structured to meet both rating agencies' minimum ratings criteria. Some CLOs will have all debt tranches rated by two rating agencies, while some will have only one. Again, it depends on the requirements of the CLO's Note investors. Some investors in CLO BB Notes may not need a rating. However, the tranche will still be rated because secondary liquidity would be harmed if the tranche was not rated.

The CLO's arranger works with the rating agencies to get the CLO's Notes rated. And it's the CLO equity that bears the cost of the ratings, and the CLO's other operating expenses.

While the leveraged loan ratings will affect the CLO's many tests, it's important to realize that the CLO manager needs to buy good leveraged loans. That is how the CLO manager earns its fee.

The CLO managers are often trying to buy/sell leveraged loans that they believe are not rated correctly by the rating agencies. Perhaps a B-rated loan that the manager thinks is of BB quality would be appealing for the CLO. When rating agencies change their ratings on a loan, especially a downgrade to CCC, the loan price can move dramatically.

CLO Notes default are tracked by the rating agencies. Below are some recent defaults.

Deal Name	Tranche	Tranche Closing Date	Original Rating	Impairment Year
Cutwater 2014-I, Ltd.	Class D	Jul-14	Ba3	2020
Cutwater 2014-I, Ltd.	Class E	Jul-14	B2	2020
Cutwater 2014-II, Ltd.	Class D	Jan-15	Ba3	2020
Halcyon Loan advisors Funding 2014-1 Ltd.	Class F	Mar-14	B2	2020
Halcyon Loan advisors Funding 2014-2 Ltd.	Class D	Apr-14	Ba3	2020
Halcyon Loan advisors Funding 2014-3 Ltd.	Class E-1	Sep-14	Ba3	2020
Halcyon Loan advisors Funding 2014-3 Ltd.	Class E-2	Sep-14	Ba3	2020
Halcyon Loan advisors Funding 2015-1 Ltd.	Class E	Apr-15	Ba3	2020
Halcyon Loan advisors Funding 2015-1 Ltd.	Class F	Apr-15	B3	2020
Halcyon Loan advisors Funding 2015-3 Ltd.	Class D	Sep-15	Ba3	2020
HarbourView CLO VII-R, Ltd.	Class F	Jun-18	B3	2020
JFIN CLO 2014-II Ltd.	Class E	Jul-14	B2	2020
Jamestown CLO V Ltd.	Class F	Dec-14	B2	2020
Trinitas CLO III, Ltd.	Class F	Jun-15	B2	2020
WhiteHorse IX, Ltd.	Class F	Jul-14	B2	2020
Halcyon Loan advisors Funding 2013-2 Ltd.	Class E	Jul-13	Ba3	2020
JFIN CLO 2015 Ltd.	Class E	Apr-15	Ba3	2020
JFIN CLO 2015 Ltd.	Class F	Apr-15	B2	2020
HarbourView CLO VII-R, Ltd.	Class E	Jun-18	Ba3	2020
Halcyon Loan advisors Funding 2015-2 Ltd.	Class F	Jun-15	B3	2020

Source: Moody's Investor Service

The rating agencies are also a good source of information for what's happening in the leveraged loan/CLO markets. Two market outlooks are included below.

MACROECONOMIC UNCERTAINTY WILL WEIGH ON US CLO SECTORS IN 2023

Fri 16 Dec, 2022 - 2:59 PM ET

Related Content: U.S. Corporates CLO Sector-Level Outlooks 2023

Fitch Ratings-Chicago-16 December 2022: The global macroeconomic slowdown will be a headwind for U.S. collateralized loan obligations in 2023, given the outlook for various corporate sectors, says Fitch Ratings. Cost pressures are expected to ease as supply chain challenges subside and inflation starts to normalize, but revenue growth will continue to slow and the upward trajectory for interest rates may persist.

Fitch's December 2022 U.S. economic forecast incorporates a mild recession in 2023, with quarterly GDP declining 0.6% in 2Q23 and 0.7% 3Q23. We currently expect the policy interest rate to rise to 5% by March 2023 and hold there for the rest of the year as inflation subsides.

The mix of outlooks for corporate CLO sectors is roughly 50% deteriorating and 50% neutral. Key watch items for 2023 include top-line pressure due to demand erosion and weaker pricing as the economy weakens, margin trends as supply chain issues and inflation subside, the trajectory of interest rates, FCF generation and default rates.

However, as highlighted in Fitch's recently published U.S. Leveraged Finance Outlook 2023, our 2023 outlook for U.S. Leveraged Finance is deteriorating on the back of concerns about the effects of a recession, inflation uncertainty and tightening credit markets. Collateralized loan obligations (CLOs) remain the dominant source of demand for institutional term loans, holding 64% of institutional loans outstanding at the end of 3Q22. Fitch projects the loan default rate will be 2.0%–3.0%.

NON-RATING ACTION COMMENTARY

US Leveraged Finance 2023 Outlook Deteriorating: Defaults Rise on Uncertainty

Tue 13 Dec, 2022 - 2:12 PM ET

Related Content: U.S. Leveraged Finance Outlook 2023

Fitch Ratings-Toronto/New York-13 December 2022: The outlook for U.S. Leveraged Finance in 2023 is deteriorating, according to Fitch Ratings. This reflects Fitch's individual sector outlooks weighted by their size in the market, default rate expectations and overall economic conditions, including recession and inflation uncertainty.

Fitch's 2023 default rate expectations are 2.5%–3.5% for high-yield bonds and 2%–3% for institutional loans, showing growing macroeconomic headwinds, such as the mild U.S. recession Fitch expects to occur in mid-2023 and 0.2% GDP growth. Several larger high-yield defaults will likely be concentrated in the retail, telecommunications and broadcast media spaces.

All sectors but one, aerospace and defense, are expecting neutral or deteriorating conditions in 2023 relative to 2022. Technology, the largest leveraged finance sector, has a deteriorating outlook due to expectations for weaker hardware and software demand. Other large sectors, such as healthcare and pharmaceuticals, business services and energy have neutral outlooks.

The percentage of broadly syndicated issuers with Stable Rating Outlooks stands at 77%, up just 1% from 2021. The distribution is similar for middle-market issuers, with Stable Outlooks increasing marginally to 87% for 2022. Issuers with Negative Outlooks or on Negative Watch are approximately 10% and 8% for broadly syndicated loan issuers and middle-market issuers, respectively.

Fitch expects middle-market firms to be more vulnerable to headwinds in 2023, which could result in elevated default rates as high as 5.0%, up from 1.1% in 2022 and exceeding the 2.0%–3.0% expected for the broad syndicated loan segment for 2023.

Source: Fitch Ratings

3.4 CLO Trustee

The CLO trustee performs several functions. The trustee is the custodian for all the CLO's leveraged loans and cash. The CLO manager does not handle the CLO's cash; that protects the CLO's investors because it limits the probability of fraud. The trustee ensures that the CLO's indenture is closely followed. The trustee sends the CLO's various investors the cash they're due each quarter. The CLO's monthly trustee reports and quarterly payment reports are produced by a collaboration between the trustee and the CLO manager.

From the perspective of a CLO equity or BB Note investor, usually, the choice of trustee is not an important item. A recent ranking of CLO Trustees is shown below.

Global Trustee Rankings — 2022

Rank	Trustee	($bn)	Deals
1	US Bank	60.2	134
2	BNY Mellon	36.6	85
3	Citibank	25.8	55
4	Deutsche Bank	14.8	33
5	Computershare	5.3	10

Source: Creditflux

CLO Financing Structure

4.1 The Simplified Bank

Thus far, the CLO's leveraged loans and the various CLO market participants have been described. Now let's analyze how the CLO is financed. Let's start with the CLO's basic structure and fill in the pieces from there.

Assets	Liabilities and Equity
$500 million First Lien Loans Floating Rate Secured by Assets of the Company Private Equity-Owned Borrowers	Investment Grade Debt $430 million BB Notes - $20 million First Loss Equity - $50 million

Usually, the CLO will issue notes in tranches rated AAA, AA, A, BBB, BB, and equity to purchase the CLO's leveraged loans. Occasionally a single B-rated tranche will also be issued. The AAA is the largest tranche the CLO issues accounting for approximately 65% of the total financing of the CLO. Combining all the CLO Notes allows you to finance 90% of the CLO's leveraged loans and equity finances the remaining 10%.

A key concept in CLOs is that the CLO's financing rate is highly correlated to the rate an investor earns on the leveraged loans.

That is because most leveraged loans are bought by CLOs. If the leveraged loans pay a high spread vs. historical levels, the CLO can afford to pay a higher borrowing cost to finance the leveraged loans.

Relationship Between the Spreads of Leveraged Loans and AAA Notes

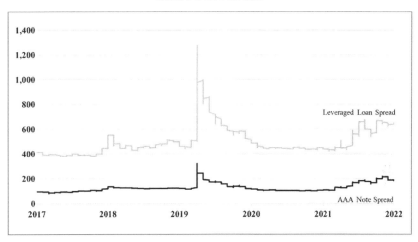

Source: Credit Suisse Leveraged Loan Index Discount Margin and Palmer Square CLO AAA Index Discount Margin

A detailed breakdown of a CLO's financing structure is shown below.

Detailed Sample CLO Financing Structure 2020 Vintage

Security	Amount	Moody's Rating	Par Sub	Base Rate	Spread/ Coupon	Discount Margin	Price	Proceeds
Class A1 Senior Notes	[228,000,000]	[Aaa]	[36.00%]	3M LIBOR	[139]	[139]	[100.00%]	[228,000,000]
Class A2 Senior Notes	[28,000,000]	[Aaa]	[36.00%]	Fixed	[3.294%]	[134]	[100.00%]	[28,000,000]
Class B Senior Notes	[48,000,000]	[Aa2]	[24.00%]	3M LIBOR	[190]	[190]	[100.00%]	[48,000,000]
Class C Mezzanine Notes	[24,000,000]	[A2]	[18.00%]	3M LIBOR	[250]	[255]	[100.00%]	[24,000,000]
Class D Mezzanine Notes	[24,000,000]	[Baa3]	[12.00%]	3M LIBOR	[365]	[365]	[100.00%]	[24,000,000]
Class E Junior Notes	[16,000,000]	[Ba3]	[8.00%]	3M LIBOR	[747]	[780]	[98.00%]	[15,680,000]
CLO Equity (Sub Notes)	[35,000,000]	[NR]					[88.75%]	[31,062,500]
Total	[403,000,000]					[195] bps		[398,742,500]

The reason for the disparity in ratings and spread between the different CLO Notes is the AAA tranche's seniority over more junior tranches in what is called the CLO payment waterfall.

The tranches rated AAA are sold to banks and insurance companies, who earn a rate of SOFR + ~2.0% as of the end of 2022.

Banks used to invest directly in leveraged loans, but now they prefer to own AAA and AA Notes issued by CLOs. These investments earn a lower interest rate than the leveraged loans but have a lower probability of default. That means the bank sets aside less regulatory capital for the AAA Note than the leveraged loan. In this manner, the bank can optimize its return on equity, a key performance metric for banks' shareholders.

The junior-most note issued by the CLO, usually the BB Note, had a rate of SOFR + ~9.8% as of the end of 2022. These notes are bought by hedge funds, alternative asset managers, interval funds, and high yield bond funds. Occasionally, CLOs will issue a B Note at ~2.0% above the cost of the BB note. The rationale for issuing this note is described in Section 13.10.

As the leveraged loans in a CLO make their interest payments, the AAA is the first note to receive the cash flow until its interest is paid in full. Then the AA gets paid its interest. And so it goes until the BB gets paid its interest. The CLO manager also needs to be remunerated. The fee is around 40 bps, usually split into a senior and junior position in the waterfall. The CLO equity doesn't have a contractual interest rate; rather, it receives all the cash flow not used to satisfy the CLO's more senior claimants.

Cash Recived From Interest On The CLO's Loans

less: Senior Collateral Management Fee

less: AAA interest

less: AA interest

less: A interest

less: BBB interest

less: BB interest

less: Junior Collateral Manager Fee

Increasing Risk and Return

Remainder To The Equity Tranche

Because of the priority of payments shown above, the various CLO Notes have different levels of risk and return. Shown below, the CLO Notes that are higher in the priority of payments receive higher ratings and offer lower returns over LIBOR or SOFR.

Historical Discount Margins for CLO Notes

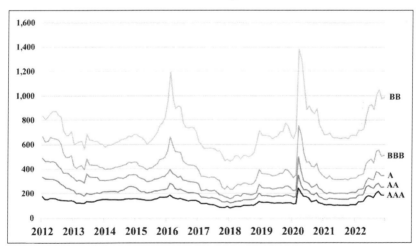

Source: Palmer Square CLO Indices

An investor in the AAA Note is taking relatively little risk; it's assumed that the probability of default on this note is almost zero. In fact, there have been no defaults on any AAA Notes. An investor in the AAA Note probably considers his or her biggest risk a downgrade in ratings or an illiquid market when at a time he or she wants to sell. Investors in AAA Notes usually prefer CLOs managed by large firms, where dramatic changes to the credit team are considered unlikely. These managers also have the most liquidity in the secondary market. If an investor is willing to take a chance on a less-well-regarded CLO manager, the AAA rates are 10 to 20 bps higher.

An investor in the BB Note is taking more risk given the more junior position in the waterfall. Still, the investor probably thinks the default probability of the tranche is remote. After all, initially, 8% or more equity is subordinated to the BB Note.

The first defaults in the CLO are, of course, absorbed by the equity tranche. The equity tranche takes this risk in exchange for high cash distributions. The extent of losses on the CLO's leveraged loans will be the biggest driver of the returns of the equity tranche. In most reasonable scenarios, leveraged loan losses would not rise to the rate where there is an impairment on any of the CLO's Notes.

The debt tranches used to finance the CLO are executed on favorable terms for the CLO equity. While the CLO's leveraged loans are often traded and priced by banks, there are no mark-to-market margining or forced sale provisions in the CLO. If the leveraged loans trade down in price, the distributions to the equity will continue, provided there aren't too many defaults or CCC/Caa-rated leveraged loans. The CLO's financing is long-term, with most CLO's having a projected life of over eight years. Because the debt is placed on such favorable terms for the CLO's equity, it's often considered an asset. After all, if the CLO's financing is not executed on attractive terms, there wouldn't be a reason for anyone to invest in a CLO equity tranche.

4.2 Overcollateralization Tests

The buyers of CLO Notes receive material structural protections; otherwise, the rating agencies wouldn't assign them the ratings they do. Although CLOs don't have mark-to-market margining or forced sale provisions, CLOs are still required to maintain compliance with important tests such as par value or Over Collateralization (O/C) test. The O/C test compares the CLO's par value of performing loans vs. the amount of debt issued by the CLO. Below is an example of a 2021 vintage CLO O/C test calculation:

Example O/C Tests and Cushions

Tranche	Coupon	Rating	Par Value of CLO Loans (Numerator)	CLO Debt Amount	Denominator of O/C Test	O/C Test Result	Required O/C	Cushion
A1	.IBOR_3MO + 1.0	AAA/AAA	500,688,729	290,000,000				
A2	.IBOR_3MO + 1.4	-/AAA	500,688,729	35,000,000				
B	.IBOR_3MO + 1.6	AA/-	500,688,729	55,000,000	380,000,000	131.80%	121.60%	10.20%
C	.IBOR_3MO + 1.9	A/-	500,688,729	31,000,000	411,000,000	121.80%	113.70%	8.20%
D	.IBOR_3MO + 3.0	BBB/-	500,688,729	29,000,000	440,000,000	113.80%	107.60%	6.20%
E	.IBOR_3MO + 5.7	BB/-	500,688,729	20,000,000	460,000,000	108.80%	104.90%	3.90%
Equity	N/A	-/-	500,688,729	51,600,000				

This CLO has two AAA-rated tranches, with the A2 junior to the A1. There are no O/C tests for the AAA notes because no tranches are senior to the AAA.

The senior-most O/C test is applied to the $55 million AA Note. The numerator of the Class B O/C test is the par value of leveraged loans, adjusted downward when there are excess CCC/Caa-rated or defaulted leveraged loans. The denominator of the O/C test is the principal balance of the Class B plus all notes senior to the

Class B (in this case, the classes A1 and A2). The par balance of leveraged loans is $500.7 million, so the Class B O/C test ratio is $500.7 million / ($290 million + $35 million + $55 million) = 131.8%. The CLO's required ratio is 121.6%, so the deal passes this O/C test. That means the CLO's waterfall will allow interest to be paid on notes junior to the Class B. The O/C test ratios that pertain to debt less senior than the class B are naturally lower as more debt is included in the ratio's denominator while the numerator remains the same. In the example above, the most junior O/C test passed by a cushion of 3.9%. Assuming a 30% loss when a leveraged loan defaults, the CLO would need to see a default rate of 13% (3.9%/30%) before the CLO's equity distributions are disrupted. This assumes the CLO manager does not buy loans below par to compensate for some of the losses.

While the denominators of the O/C tests are fixed using the debt outstanding for that particular note, the numerator can be adjusted downward if significant credit deterioration exists in the leveraged loans. Most importantly, if a leveraged loan defaults, it's no longer carried at par value. Its carrying value is the lower of the current market value and a hypothetical recovery value assigned by a rating agency.

Leveraged loans rated CCC/Caa that exceed 7.5% of the portfolio can also haircut the par balance of leveraged loans. For example, in a CLO with 8.6% CCC-rated leveraged loans, the 1.1% of CCC-rated CLO loan assets above the limit would be carried at market value. The leveraged loans used to haircut the CCC-rated bucket are those with the lowest market value. In the example below, the CLO has an excess CCC-rated amount. The numerator of the O/C test is reduced by the mark-to-market losses of Company C and E.

Example Excess CCC Ratio Calculation

Loan	S&P Rating	Par Balance ($)	% Of Par	Market Price	Market to Market Loss ($)
Company A	CCC	6,000,000	1.20%	100.00%	-
Company B	CCC	5,500,000	1.10%	89.00%	605,000
Company C	CCC	4,000,000	0.80%	70.00%	1,200,000
Company D	CCC	4,500,000	0.90%	84.00%	720,000
Company E	CCC	5,000,000	1.00%	68.00%	1,600,000
Company F	CCC	6,250,000	1.25%	96.00%	250,000
Company G	CCC	5,700,000	1.14%	99.00%	57,000
Company H	CCC	6,250,000	1.25%	100.00%	
Total		43,200,000			
CCC % of Par		8.63%			
CCC % Threshold		7.50%			
CCC % Excess		1.13%			
Worst CCC by price					
Company E		5,000,000	1.00%	68.00%	1,600,000
Company C		4,000,000	0.80%	70.00%	1,200,000
Reduction in Par Balance for O/C Test					2,800,000

Moody's will also have a similar test, and whichever rating agency produces the largest reduction in the par balance of leveraged loans will usually be the haircut used by the CLO. If the CLO fails the test above, it will be prohibited from buying another CCC-rated asset. The CLO manager may want to sell Company A's leveraged loan at par to reduce the excess CCC bucket. But, CCC-rated loans generally have high spreads that the CLO manager may not want to remove from the portfolio.

Newly issued CLOs may have 2–3% CCC/Caa-rated leveraged loans, so the example above shows significant negative credit migration. This example would probably correspond to a CLO in a recessionary period or a seasoned CLO.

As the CLO's leveraged loans show deterioration, one test will fail before the O/C test. This is the interest diversion test, and its cushion is slightly lower than the junior-most O/C test. When this test fails, the CLO takes up to 50% of the cash flow that would have otherwise been paid to the equity and instead uses it to purchase additional leveraged loans. This puts the CLO's Note investors in a better position, as they're secured by more collateral. It's also not the worst thing for the CLO's equity, because the newly purchased leveraged loans will pay interest into the CLO's payment waterfall, and the CLO's equity should ultimately recover value from these leveraged loans when the CLO is liquidated. Regardless, tripping this test would not be fun for the CLO's equity investors, as they probably did not expect to see unfavorable performance of the leveraged loans. Most investors in CLOs are aligning themselves with CLO managers whom they expect to pass these tests.

If excess Caa/CCC-rated assets and defaults rise to a level where an O/C test is failing, the distributions to the equity are stopped. Cash flow otherwise payable to the equity is used to repay the senior-most outstanding CLO Note until the O/C test comes back into compliance. Any interest due but unpaid on the CLO's Notes is capitalized into its principal balance. But there is no event of default. Unfortunately for the CLO's equity, when this happens, the CLO repays its lowest-cost debt, and there isn't an ability to re-borrow. A surprising result of the CLO's rules is that the worse the CLO's leveraged loans perform, the sooner the AAA Note begins getting repaid.

One thing that may surprise someone new to CLOs is that when a leveraged loan is purchased for a price above 80 to 85 cents on the dollar, the leveraged loan is carried at the full par balance for purposes of the O/C test. Thus, the O/C test initially appears to be a test that's easy to game by buying leveraged loans that are trading at discounts to par value. But buying discounted leveraged loans can be risky, as the discounted loans imply a higher risk of default or downgrade. If the discounted loans default, the manager has moved the problem into the future but also compounded the problem.

4.3 Interest Coverage Tests

CLOs also have interest coverage tests, which function the same way as O/C tests. They measure the amount of interest received on the leveraged loans compared to the interest due on the CLO's Notes. In my experience, it's more likely that the O/C tests fail when the quality of the CLO's leveraged loans deteriorates. Usually, the manager will buy leveraged loans with enough spread to satisfy interest coverage tests. The consequences of failing an I/C test are the same as for an O/C test, cash flows to the equity or possibly the BB note are diverted.

4.4 Collateral Quality Tests

There are collateral quality tests in a CLO, but these tests are less critical than the O/C or I/C tests described above. That's because the CLO can fail these tests, but cash flows in the CLO waterfall are unaffected. Collateral quality tests are measured on a maintain or improve basis. That means the CLO manager cannot buy a leveraged loan that would push the CLO further into failing a test. For example, if the Moody's diversity test (explained below) is failing, the CLO manager cannot buy a new loan that would lower the test result.

Weighted Average Life (WAL) Test

In practice, this test governs how long a CLO can stay fully invested. The weighted average life test maximum might begin at nine years and step down by 0.25 years every quarter. Five years into the life of the CLO, the collateral manager will have a weighted average life test limit of four years, so each new loan acquired must have less than four years until maturity. As this test limit ratchets down, there will be fewer and fewer loans that are eligible for purchase by the CLO. When that happens, the CLO will begin amortizing or could possibly be reset into a new CLO.

A longer weighted average life test cushion is generally favorable for CLO equity because it gives the CLO more time to make distributions and possibly build gains and incremental spread on the leveraged loans. However, a longer weighted average life test usually commands a higher purchase price for the equity, all things being equal. Conversely, a shorter life CLO may be closer to the expiration of the non-call period, which could provide options for pickup in equity value. For the CLO BB Note investor, a shorter weighted average life is beneficial, as it means there is less time for the leveraged loans to lose material value.

Weighted Average Rating Factor

The Weighted Average Rating Factor (WARF) is a key collateral quality test for CLOs with Notes rated by Moody's. For WARF, the lower number indicates higher overall leveraged loan quality. The ratings scale is exponential, and if ratings decline by one notch, the corresponding ratings factor increases materially. The scale below shows how beneficial it's to add some BB-rated leveraged loans to the portfolio while holding Caa-rated assets is detrimental to the WARF ratio. Many CLO portfolios have WARFs in the 2,800 range, slightly worse than B2 on average.

Moody's Rating	Moody's Rating Factor	Moody's Rating	Moody's Rating Factor
Aaa	1	Ba1	940
Aa1	10	Ba2	1,350
Aa2	20	Ba3	1,766
Aa3	40	B1	2,220
A1	70	B2	2,720
A2	120	B3	3,490
A3	180	Caa1	4,770
Baa1	260	Caa2	6,500
Baa2	360	Caa3	8,070
Baa3	610	Ca-C	10,000

While this test is important, in my experience, the amount of leveraged loans trading at stressed levels is the better test for leveraged loan portfolio quality. Rating agency opinions may be stale or unreflective of the underlying risks in the loans. For example, if a leveraged loan is trading at 80 cents on the dollar, that provides critical information of how risky the leveraged loan is, and daily price changes can be monitored.

Diversity Score

A diversified leveraged loan portfolio is a requirement for a CLO. Without it, there isn't any way the CLO could obtain the ratings it does for its Senior Notes, nor would CLO arrangers be able to find Senior Note investors interested in participating in the CLO. For example, the CLO BB Note begins its life with a minimum of 8% equity, which takes the first loss on the loan portfolio. If one leveraged loan loss could eat through most of the equity capital, that would make the CLO BB Note a risky investment. But if each leveraged loan was less than 1% of the CLO's assets, the CLO BB Note is in a much better position.

Diversity is a mixed bag for the equity investor. On the one hand, investors in the CLO's Notes like higher diversity CLO managers and award them lower financing costs, which benefit CLO equity cash flows. On the other hand, equity investors may prefer a less diverse portfolio with high-conviction investments that may be higher spread. High diversity levels indicate a "buying the market" investment strategy that may not be worth the management fee charged by the CLO manager.

There will also be concentration limits for the largest leveraged loan owned by the CLO (1–2% of total assets) and maximum industry concentrations (10–15% of assets). The largest industry concentrations in CLOs are usually healthcare, technology, and business services. The CLO manager has considerable leeway in deciding industry categorization and some business models could easily fit into several different industry classifications. It's not uncommon to see different managers assign different industry categories to the loans they own.

Recovery Rate

Both Moody's and S&P assign a recovery rating to the loans that go into the CLO. This rating is on a separate scale from the ratings detailed in Section 3.3 above. The recovery rate represents how well a lender is likely to do if the business goes into bankruptcy. A business with hard assets will likely receive a higher recovery rating than one with more intangible assets.

Weighted Average Spread Test

The higher the test result, the better. This test works in a way that might seem counterintuitive, as low-spread portfolios imply lower leveraged loan risk. However, the CLOs must have a minimum spread to ensure that the Senior Note interest expense can be comfortably serviced.

The Maximum CCC/Caa test

Most CLOs allow for 7.5% of the portfolio to be rated CCC or Caa. As discussed in Section 4.4, CCC/Caa-rated loans in excess of 7.5% are held at fair market value for purposes of the O/C tests. For a CLO that has not had substantial leveraged loan losses, failing the CCC/Caa won't jeopardize CLO equity cash flows because there are excess performing leveraged loans in the CLO.

Below are several collateral quality tests:

Collateral Quality Test	Actual	Required	Passing	Notes
Weighted Average Ratings Factor	2,824	2,889	yes	Moody's calculates the weighted average ratings of the CLO loan assets. A B2 rating is equivalent to 2,720 and a B3 rating is equivalent to 3,490
Moody's Diversity	75	65	yes	The diversity test is optimized by having the largest number of borrowers in the largest number of industries
Caa or less %	2.60%	7.50%	yes	If Caa exceeds the cap the CLO's O/C test will be negatively effected
CCC+ or less %	3.50%	7.50%	yes	If CCC exceeds the cap the CLO's O/C test will be negatively effected
Weighted Average Spread	3.50%	3.20%	yes	The weighted average spread of the CLO loan assets needs to exceed a minimum so that the CLO's interest expense can be comfortably serviced
Weighted Average Life	4.9	6.5	yes	The weighted average life or maturity of the CLO loan assets declines over time so that eventually the CLO won't be able to buy new loans and the CLO will begin to amortize
S&P Recovery Rate	46	44	yes	S&P assigns a hypothetical recovery rate for each leveraged loan
Moody's Recovery Rate	49	43	yes	Moody's assigns a hypothetical recovery rate for each leveraged loan

4.5 Market Value Analytics

The prices of leveraged loans change daily, and two market value metrics correspond to CLO investments. For CLO Notes, Market Value O/C ("MVOC") is the relevant metric. This is the calculation for two of the debt tranches:

$$AAA\ MVOC = (fair\ market\ value\ of\ all\ loans + cash) / total\ balance\ of\ AAA\ notes\ only$$

$$BB\ MVOC = (fair\ market\ value\ of\ all\ loans + cash) / total\ balance\ of\ AAA\ to\ BB\ notes$$

The denominator always includes the specific note of the MVOC you are interested in and all CLO Notes senior to that tranche (but excluding the X Note when applicable). Obviously, a higher MVOC is more desirable for the noteholder, as there is a greater fair market value of leveraged loans compared to the CLO Notes.

For the CLO's equity investor, the NAV is the relevant concept. The NAV represents the cash proceeds to the equity tranche if the CLO were liquidated on that date. The NAV should exclude any income accrued on the loan portfolio or the CLO's notes; the profitability of the CLO is considered separate from the NAV.

Equity NAV = (fair market value of all leveraged loans + cash – all CLO Notes less the X Note when applicable)/CLO Equity total amount.

For a new CLO, the equity NAV starts around 70%. That's because the CLO has upfront costs borne by the equity including: lawyers, rating agencies, and an arranger fee. Over time the NAV will change based on the fair market value of the underlying leveraged loans. A small move in leveraged loan prices will be magnified by ~10x at the equity tranche level, given the embedded leverage in the CLO.

A Bloomberg terminal has the daily NAVs of most CLOs, and any CLO broker dealer can supply the same information using their own systems. An example is shown below:

Sample Net Asset Value Calculation for 2020 Vintage CLO at Year End 2022

Class	Amount	% Bal	% Sub	Coupon %	MVOC	Par OC
A1A1	1,123,881	59.5%	40.5%	5.9	158.3%	166.0%
A1B	107,000	5.7%	34.8%	6.2	144.6%	151.6%
A2	171,000	9.1%	25.7%	6.6	126.9%	133.1%
B	121,000	6.4%	19.3%	6.8	116.8%	122.5%
C	117,000	6.2%	13.1%	7.8	108.5%	113.8%
D	86,000	4.6%	8.6%	10.8	103.1%	108.1%
SUB	161,750	8.6%	0.0%	0.0	33.1%	86.6%

According to the data above, this CLO has a portfolio market value of $1.78 billion (one of the biggest CLOs). After subtracting the principal amount of CLO Notes, the CLO's equity (referred to as "sub notes") has 33.1% of its principal balance. If all the leveraged loans were to recover par value, the CLO equity would receive 86.6%. While this is not likely, it's good to know that there is some upside to the current NAV if leveraged loans increase in price.

4.6 Loan Loss Reserve

One of the important ways that CLO equity is different from other lending-based asset classes is that CLO analysts factor in a loss reserve to their expected CLO equity returns. That's because even the best CLO managers will inevitably choose some leveraged loans that default. The loss reserve is not cash in an account at the CLO trustee. Rather, it's a discounting of the returns the CLO equity is projected to provide by including some defaults into the equation. For example, a CLO equity tranche might offer a 20% return if no loans ever default and a 15% return if the leveraged loan default rate approximates historical levels. CLO equity investors would focus on the 15% return and consider the zero-default return case largely unattainable.

Most CLO equity analysts calculate the loan loss reserve assuming 2% of the loans will default each year, and the loan recovery rate will be 70%. Therefore, the annual loss rate is 60 bps [2% × (100% − 70%)]. Additional loss reserves are taken for loans trading below 90, as those are more susceptible to default. But why are these the chosen numbers?

The default and recovery data shown in Section 2.10 show a historical default rate of 3.0% with a recovery rate of 65% for a 1.05% loss rate [3% × (100% − 65%)]. But this is overly pessimistic for two reasons.

First, the recovery rate used in the data set is the trading price of the loan thirty days after default. The CLO manager could sell the leveraged loan prior to default when financial results are not as dire. In addition, they could hold the leveraged loan through a restructuring, in anticipation of receiving proceeds greater than the trading price thirty days after default. The CLO does not have provisions requiring a CLO manager to sell a defaulted asset.

Second, CLO managers are picking leveraged loans that are more conservative than the overall Loan Index. For example, at year-end 2022, the estimated Credit Suisse Leveraged Loan Index spread was LIBOR + 3.90%. However, most CLOs have weighted average spreads of LIBOR + 3.50% or lower. Business Development Companies or hedge funds often buy the riskiest loans in the leveraged loan market; these loans would not be appropriate for a CLO employing leverage of 10.0x.

When factoring in gains from buying leveraged loans at a discount, the implied default rate in CLOs has been only 43.9% of the total default rate in the Loan Index.

CLO Defaults vs. Loan Index Defaults

Vintage	# of CLOs	Change in par value of loans	Cumulative defaults assuming 65% recovery	4 year index cumulative defaults	CLO default rate / index default rate
2012	83	0.2%		10.0%	
2013	91	-1.3%	3.7%	10.0%	37.1%
2014	106	-1.7%	4.9%	10.0%	48.6%
2015	82	-0.9%	2.6%	8.0%	32.1%
2016	47	-2.0%	5.7%	10.0%	57.1%
2017	76	-1.4%	4.0%	9.0%	44.4%
Average					43.9%

Source: Nomura CLO Research; newer CLOs are excluded because they are not terminated

If the Loan Index loss rate is 1.05%, the implied loss rate in CLO portfolios is only 46 bps (1.05% * 43.9%). But the 60 bps loan loss reserve is not netted for loan gains. If a CLO analyst assumes that 25% of the leveraged loans prepay each year and new leveraged loans are purchased at 99.5, that implies 13 bps of annual loan gains [(25% * [1-99.5%)]. Loan losses of 60 bps less loan gains of 13 bps result in 47 bps of net leveraged loan losses, which ties very close to the data above.

It should be noted that leveraged loan recoveries have experienced a negative trend. Today a greater proportion of leveraged loans are first lien only. If there is no second lien loan or high yield bond in a company's financing structure, the first lien loan-to-value is higher, and a potential recovery in a restructuring is lower; there is no junior debt buffer to feel the pain along with the equity in the restructuring.

The broadly syndicated leveraged loan market is mainly covenant-lite. That means borrowers are not required to negotiate with lenders before a payment default to try to fix the company's business issues. When a payment default happens, it may mean that the company's enterprise value has deteriorated significantly. However, covenant-lite loans may default less often.

4.7 Fixed Rate Tranches

A CLO will often have a CLO Note that is fixed rate instead of floating. However, this introduces basis risk to the CLO as almost all the CLO's assets will be floating. As a result, the rating agencies will limit the amount of fixed-rate CLO Note issuance to usually less than 5% of the CLO's financing. When a CLO is forming, fixed-rate tranches can be negotiated by taking a floating rate of interest and swapping those cash flows into a fixed rate. However, the CLO's equity investor would usually not want to finance the CLO with the actual swap rate. The CLO equity would require the fixed-rate note to be sold at a lower rate than the actual swap rate because the CLO equity investor would not want to introduce basis risk to the CLO.

In the CLO below, three different tranches of fixed-rate notes were sold. If you look at tranche A1, the spread is three-month SOFR + 2.45%; there is also a fixed rate trance, AF, which has the same seniority and pays a 5% fixed rate. The fixed-rate tranche was introduced either because the fixed rate was lower than the expected floating rate payments of A1 or because the CLO arranger needed to issue $26 million of fixed-rate notes to get the CLO financed.

2021 Vintage Middle Market CLO

Tranche	Coupon	Floater Formula	Original Ratings	Current Balance
X	4.9000	Fixed	AAA	17,500,000
A1	5.6262	SOFR_3MO + 2.45	AAA	31,750,000
AF	5.0000	Fixed	AAA	26,000,000
AL	5.6262	SOFR_3MO + 2.45	AAA	40,000,000
B1	6.6762	SOFR_3MO + 3.50	AA	27,000,000
BF	5.9800	Fixed	AA	8,000,000
C	7.9262	SOFR_3MO + 4.75	A-	32,375,000
D	9.5962	SOFR_3MO + 6.42	BBB-	19,250,000
E	12.6762	SOFR_3MO + 9.50	BB-	24,000,000
Equity				52,700,000

4.8 The X Note

In the CLO Financing above, there is a large X Note at $17.5 million. The X Note is a CLO Note like no other. That is because it has scheduled amortization over one to three years. Other CLO Notes do not have scheduled amortization; their full principal remains outstanding until the CLO is called or leveraged loans prepayments deleverage the CLO. The X Note is paid with cash flow that would have otherwise gone to the CLO equity. In general, the issuance of an X Note should be accretive to the CLO equity because the X Note has an interest rate below that of the projected CLO equity returns.

The X Note can be issued in a new CLO, which would add inexpensive leverage. But the most common use of X Notes is in a reset transaction. Let's say a CLO began its life a few years ago, and the CLO equity investor wants to extend the CLO's reinvestment period. It's expected that a few years into the CLO's life, there could be some losses on the CLO's leveraged loans. In that case, additional equity will be needed to convince new CLO Note investors to want to continue financing the CLO's leveraged loans. The X Note can be issued to buy more leveraged loans, effectively increasing the collateral for the CLO Note investors. The X Note is a much simpler solution than finding all the CLO's equity investors and asking them to contribute additional equity to the CLO in proportion to their equity ownership.

Once the X Note is repaid, the CLO Equity investors begin receiving their full equity distributions, and there is less debt financing the CLO.

4.9 The Fee Rebate Letter

In some cases, the CLO manager will give the CLO's equity investors a fee rebate letter. This is a several-page contract that entitles the CLO's equity investor to a portion of the CLO's management fee. If the CLO management fee in the CLO's indenture is 45 bps per annum, the side letter may discount management fees to 35 bps per annum. An investor in CLO equity may prefer the indenture to have the 35 bps management fee, as this is the most straightforward method to rebate. The 10 bps decrease in management fee equals about 1.0% of additional cash flow to the equity at 10x leverage.

The CLO manager may prefer the management fee rebate to be accomplished via a side letter (outside the indenture) for two reasons. First, the fee rebate letter allows for the private discounting of the management fee, while the indenture shows the full management fee to other market participants. That may help the CLO manager negotiate a higher fee on its next CLO since its previous management fee discounting isn't publicly disclosed.

The other reason side letters exist is that some equity investors may get a fee rebate letter while others do not. This reflects the relative bargaining power of the CLO's equity investors when the CLO is formed. The side letter is usually tradeable but rarely transacted in the secondary market. A secondary benefit to the CLO equity is that all cash flows associated with the management fee rebate letter are captured outside of the 12% incentive hurdle. Thus, the owner of the fee rebate letter will have a return above 12% before the incentive fee begins paying. The downside to taking the side letter is that it adds to accounting complexity as one investment becomes documented in two separate agreements.

Interest Rates

One of the challenges of modeling CLOs is that the interest payments on the CLO's leveraged loans and debt payments on the CLO's Notes are based on a floating rate of interest. In 2022, interest rates increased substantially as the Federal Reserve moved to lower inflation.

Historical Three-Month Libor

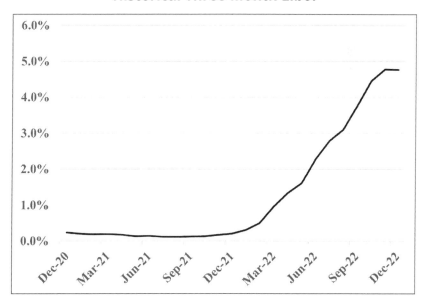

Future interest rates are unknown, but we can look to a LIBOR/SOFR forward curve for the market's implied future rates.

Forward Three-Month LIBOR

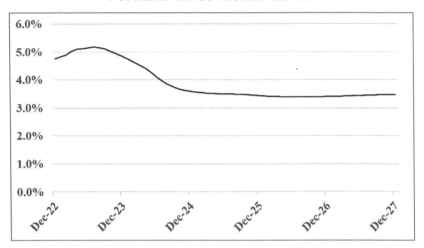

The LIBOR curve above shows that after September 2023, LIBOR is expected to normalize in the 3.5% area. Interest rates may not play out this way, but these are the best assumptions we have for future rates, and we use them in our models.

Higher LIBOR should lead to higher returns for the CLO's equity tranche. That's because the CLO has more leveraged loans than CLO notes, thus making CLO equity a floating-rate product. However, CLO equity can also thrive when interest rates are declining. When the Federal Reserve cut interest rates in 2019, investors in loan mutual funds and ETFs redeemed their shares and allocated a larger percentage of their portfolios towards fixed-rate bonds. That put downward technical pressure on leveraged loan prices and provided CLOs in their reinvestment periods with more attractive investment opportunities. Additionally, lower LIBOR means lower interest payments for the borrowers in a CLO, potentially leading to lower defaults. And when LIBOR rises, it should be a sign that the economy is doing well; in that scenario, presumably, the default rate would be expected to be low. It really is a mixed bag!

In many aspects of investing in CLOs, changing one input variable can influence returns differently from one's first intuition; second-order derivatives need to be considered.

5.1 Transition to SOFR

Prior to 2022, leveraged loans and CLO Notes used LIBOR as the underlying floating rate. However, because LIBOR was manipulated in the past, the rate will no longer exist after June 2023. The rate chosen to replace LIBOR is SOFR. LIBOR was based on polling a group of large banks to determine the rate they would pay if they borrowed from other banks. The advantage of SOFR is that it's determined by market forces. One difference between these two floating rates is that SOFR is secured, while LIBOR is not. Consequently, SOFR should be lower than LIBOR. Over the last five years, the LIBOR/SOFR basis (LIBOR – SOFR) has been 26 bps. In June 2023, the entire CLO market will be SOFR-based.

A goal of the transition from LIBOR to SOFR is ensuring that changing the base rate will not advantage or disadvantage any of the parties in the CLO. However, this may be hard to achieve in practice, and there will be some winners and losers at the margin.

Most CLO indentures require the transition from LIBOR to SOFR on the sooner of (1) June 2023 or (2) when a majority of the CLO's loans have moved to SOFR. Because the leveraged loan prepayment rate was low in 2022, June 2023 will be the transition date for most CLOs.

Loans issued in 2022 use SOFR as the base rate plus an incremental spread adjustment of 10 to 26 bps. The actual adjustment depends on the lenders' negotiating power over the company. When a LIBOR-based loan is amended, upsized, or refinanced, the base rate can change to SOFR.

CLO Notes issued in 2022 and beyond are based on SOFR. The incremental spread adjustment in most CLO indentures is 26 bps.

CLO equity cash flows could be affected at the June 2023 transition to SOFR because CLO Note investors will receive 26 bps of incremental spread on the move to SOFR, but the CLO's leveraged loans may pick up between 10 to 26 bps. As a result, investors in CLO equity are pressuring CLO managers to ensure that the spread adjustment on the leveraged loans is the same as that of the CLO Notes.

The agreed-upon transition of CLO Notes from LIBOR to SOFR + 26 bps highlights one of the most attractive aspects of the CLO equity asset class. When CLOs do the SOFR transition, most will be out of their non-call periods. If the transition to SOFR is favorable, the CLO's equity investors may decide to keep the CLO's Notes in place through the end of the CLO's reinvestment period or longer. If the CLO's transition is not economically favorable, the CLO can be refinanced, reset, or called. When a new CLO begins its life today, the note investors are committed to the current financing for what could be up to eight years. But the short non-call period of two years gives the CLO equity a valuable optionality.

5.2 LIBOR/SOFR Basis

An additional nuance to the interest rate story is that the CLO's Notes are based on three-month LIBOR or SOFR. While the CLO's leveraged loans may have a maturity of five to seven years, the borrower chooses a one-month, three-month, or six-month LIBOR/SOFR contract. At the end of the chosen contract, the company makes a cash interest payment to the CLO and the next contract to borrow. At the end of 2022, LIBOR and SOFR had upwardly sloping term curves, so the rate is marginally higher when borrowing for a longer period. Theoretically, the cost of borrowing using three consecutive one-month contracts should equal that of borrowing using one three-month contract. However, in practice, if many companies borrow at one-month LIBOR/ SOFR and the rate stays low for an extended period, the CLO equity will see marginally lower distributions because the CLO's Notes are using a higher base rate.

Three-month/One-month LIBOR basis

In the chart above, the higher basis is negative for CLO equity returns.

While both the SOFR/LIBOR conversion and the basis between one-month and three-month SOFR/LIBOR are important, these factors sit in the backseat when compared to the critical driver of CLO equity performance: the underlying loss rate on the leveraged loans.

CLO Key Terms

6.1 Documentation

When a new CLO is formed, the arranger will help negotiate the main terms of the indenture. The indenture has all the rules the CLO will follow, both material business points and extensive legalese. The indenture is written with great care as it's designed to last the entire life of the CLO without any amendments. Indeed, amending a CLO's indenture is tricky, given the number of CLO stakeholders with different objectives and interests. For many CLOs, the indenture could run 350 pages or more. Fortunately, some sections are more relevant than others for CLO equity and BB Note investors. A few sections of importance are:

- How the indenture can be amended
- Whose consent is required for things like a refinancing or a reset
- CLO payment waterfall
- Manager's ability to swap / trade underperforming leveraged loans
- Ability to reinvest after the reinvestment period ends
- Ability to distribute excess par to the equity investors ("par flush")

6.2 Indenture Amendments

Amendments to a CLO's indenture are infrequent. The primary reason noted above is that the interests of different CLO investors are wildly divergent, and any amendment would likely benefit one group over another. Also, because there is no public registry for who owns what CLO securities, it may be impossible to locate all the CLO's investors to vote on an amendment. Notices of amendments are sent through the CLO's trustee, but not everyone will respond. If a CLO amendment is approved, it's documented as a supplemental indenture.

The indenture would usually give the CLO manager, possibly with the agreement of a majority of the AAA Notes, the ability to make indenture changes deemed "immaterial." Fixing any indenture typos, inconsistencies in the indenture or changes to comply with new regulations might fall in this category.

Amendments favorable to the CLO equity tranche could include extending the reinvestment period or loosening some of the CLO's tests. The CLO Note investors would not approve these amendments. If the CLO equity investors want to change the CLO materially, they must refinance all the CLO's Notes. The result will look like a new CLO but with the same leveraged loan portfolio. To accomplish this, a CLO arranger will be hired.

6.3 Refinancings and Resets

Most new CLOs issued in 2022 have a five-year reinvestment period and a two-year non-call period on the CLO's Notes. After the non-call period, the CLO's Notes can be refinanced or reset if a majority of the equity tranche approves.

The refinancing is straightforward and can be done by tranche, meaning some tranches can stay in place with the current spread while others are refinanced at lower spread levels. Since the AAA Note is ~65% of the CLO's financing, that's the biggest potential area to save on interest expense. The cost of the AAA Note varies with overall market conditions and investor demand, especially from Japanese banks.

Imagine that a new CLO has an AAA Note cost of SOFR + 1.90%. If the market for new-issue AAA spreads has not moved in two years, it may still be possible to refinance the AAA Note at a lower rate. At that point, the CLO will have a shorter expected life, which implies lower risk for the AAA Note investor.

An arranger might charge a refinancing fee of 10 bps of the amount of the CLO Notes refinanced. For the refinancing to be economically attractive, the CLO equity investor will weigh the upfront refinancing costs with the projected interest savings. The key assumption is how long the CLO will be outstanding.

A reset is a more complicated process that involves paying off all the CLO's tranches, except for the equity. With a reset, the CLO can make additional changes to the indenture, including extending the maturity, reinvestment period, weighted average life test, and other collateral quality tests. After the CLO is reset, you have a new CLO with the existing leveraged loan portfolio.

An upsize is also possible with a reset. Fortunately for the investors in CLO equity, the fees associated with a reset are significantly lower than new-issue CLO fees. Part of the cost savings comes from the fact that the CLO's Note ratings are reaffirmed rather than assigned a brand-new rating.

A reset is a good option when a CLO is nearing the end of its life. If the CLO equity investor can reset the CLO and get lower CLO Note costs, it's a total home run. However, it may make sense to do a reset even if the cost of the CLO's Notes increases, as the extension of the CLO's life can meaningfully increase the net present value of the CLO equity's future cash flows, as the reset keeps the CLO fully invested longer. If the cost of debt rises on a reset, the equity investor can always seek to do a refinancing after the new non-call period is over.

2014 Vintage CLO Case Study

Below is an example of a CLO's capital structure evolving over its life. Each change was approved by a majority of the equity tranche, acting to increase their expected returns. The CLO underwent several changes in its capital structure since its inception in 2014, leading up to its ultimate liquidation in 2022.

The CLO was issued in 2014 with the following capital structure:

Year 2014

Security	Amount ($)	S&P Rating	Base Rate	Spread
Class A Senior Notes	504,000,000	[AAA]	3M LIBOR	148
Class B Senior Notes	90,400,000	[AA]	3M LIBOR	200
Class C Mezzanine Notes	64,000,000	[A]	3M LIBOR	285
Class D Mezzanine Notes	40,800,000	[BBB]	3M LIBOR	365
Class E Junior Notes	35,200,000	[BB]	3M LIBOR	450
CLO Equity	77,350,000	[NR]		
Total	811,750,000			193

In 2016, the equity opted to reset and upsize the CLO. This required fully refinancing the existing capital structure and adding new equity. As seen below, the weighted average cost of the CLO's financing increased from 193 to 203 bps, driven by the wider spread on the BB notes. Below is the updated capital structure.

Year 2016

Security	Amount ($)	S&P Rating	Base Rate	Spread
Class AR Senior Notes	630,000,000	[AAA]	3M LIBOR	143
Class BR Senior Notes	113,000,000	[AA]	3M LIBOR	185
Class CR Mezzanine Notes	80,000,000	[A]	3M LIBOR	250
Class DR Mezzanine Notes	51,000,000	[BBB]	3M LIBOR	435
Class ER Junior Notes	44,000,000	[BB]	3M LIBOR	754
CLO Equity	96,700,000	[NR]		
Total	1,014,700,000			203

By 2019, CLO liability pricing had tightened to the point where the equity decided to refinance the Class A through Class D notes. The E Note remained outstanding and was not refinanced, and there was no extension of the reinvestment period. Below is the capital structure following the second refinancing in 2019. Note that the size of the debt tranches remained unchanged, and only the spreads were reduced for the relevant tranches:

Year 2019

Security	Amount ($)	S&P Rating	Base Rate	Spread
Class AR2 Senior Notes	630,000,000	[AAA]	3M LIBOR	123
Class BR2 Senior Notes	113,000,000	[AA]	3M LIBOR	175
Class CR2 Mezzanine Notes	80,000,000	[A]	3M LIBOR	245
Class DR2 Mezzanine Notes	51,000,000	[BBB]	3M LIBOR	385
Class ER Junior Notes	44,000,000	[BB]	3M LIBOR	754
CLO Equity	96,700,000	[NR]		
Total	1,014,700,000			185

In late 2020, CLO liabilities had once again tightened to the point where it made sense for the equity to refinance the capital stack. In this refinancing, the E-Note was also refinanced, and F-Note (single-B rated) was added to provide the additional par subordination to the senior debt without the equity needing to upsize its commitment. Once again, the reinvestment period was not extended as part of this transaction. Below is the capital structure following the 2020 refinancing:

Year 2020

Security	Amount ($)	S&P Rating	Base Rate	Spread
Class AR3 Senior Notes	630,000,000	[AAA]	3M LIBOR	100
Class BR3 Senior Notes	113,000,000	[AA]	3M LIBOR	140
Class CR3 Mezzanine Notes	80,000,000	[A]	3M LIBOR	200
Class DR3 Mezzanine Notes	51,000,000	[BBB]	3M LIBOR	365
Class ER2 Junior Notes	42,650,000	[BB]	3M LIBOR	697
Class FR2 Mezzanine Notes	3,950,000	[B]	3M LIBOR	850
CLO Equity	96,700,000	[NR]		
Total	1,017,300,000			159

By the end of 2021, the CLO had exited its reinvestment period and was beginning to amortize its AAA Note. The equity decided to call the transaction rather than reset the deal, and the underlying loans were sold. Proceeds were used to pay down the outstanding debt tranches, and the remainder was distributed to the equity, effectively ending the CLO's life. Whether the CLO would be called or reset in a case like this depends on the quality of the leveraged loans. If a CLO can be reset with limited new equity, a reset is often the choice. If a CLO needs material changes to the leveraged loan portfolio and significantly more equity, then calling the CLO may be the more favorable option.

6.4 Par Flush

New-issue CLOs usually allow for what's called a "par flush" on the first and/or second payment date. The cap on the par flush is negotiated when the CLO is forming and usually equals 0.5% to 1.0% of the CLO. Excess par occurs when the CLO manager buys loans cheaper than initially modeled and/or leveraged loan trading gains occur. Not all CLO managers will distribute the maximum amount of excess par the indenture allows. One reason is that the CLO manager may be concerned about the increased default risk of some of the leveraged loans in the portfolio. Another reason is that the CLO manager may want to stay in the good graces of the CLO Note investors, to make it easier to get them involved in the CLO manager's future CLOs. The CLO Note holders prefer no par flush since it represents collateral that would otherwise secure their CLO Notes.

The par flush can provide a material boost to CLO equity returns. This optionality is a reason why some CLO equity investors prefer the primary CLO market to the secondary CLO market, where the par flush is no longer an option. If excess par remains in the CLO and is not distributed as a par flush, the CLO equity investors still benefit, but not as much as if the par was quickly returned to the equity investors.

In the real-world example below, the CLO begins its life with a loan target par balance of $500 million. The CLO manager bought loans at more favorable prices than originally modeled and through successful trading had built $2.2 million of excess par as of March 2022. On the CLO's first payment date in April 2022, the excess par was distributed to the CLO's equity investor, and the excess par in the deal went to zero. Additional par built after the first payment date could not be distributed to the equity.

	Sep 2021	Dec 2021	Jan 2022	Feb 2022	Mar 2022	Apr 2022	May 2022	Jun 2022
Original Balance	500,000,000	500,000,000	500,000,000	500,000,000	500,000,000	500,000,000	500,000,000	500,000,000
Current Balance	500,000,000	500,500,490	501,809,642	502,201,517	502,234,155	500,000,000	500,183,701	500,466,204
Excess Par	0	500,490	1,809,642	2,201,517	2,234,155	0	183,701	466,204
First Payment Date						X		
CLO Equity Amoun	50,000,000	50,000,000	50,000,000	50,000,000	50,000,000	50,000,000	50,000,000	50,000,000
Par Flush / Equity						4.5%		

The par flush likely represented a material upside to the CLO equity investor's initial targeted IRR, as there isn't a way to know in advance how successful the CLO's initial purchase of leveraged loans will outperform the initial model.

In my experience, CLO managers usually add some conservatism to their forecast for the weighted average purchase price of the leveraged loan portfolio so that the CLO equity investors can benefit from the par flush on the first payment date.

6.5 Reinvestment After the End of the Reinvestment Period

When analyzing a new CLO, it's important to do a word search for the phrase "after the reinvestment period" in the CLO's indenture. This language is usually in the CLO's indenture Section 12. While a CLO has a defined reinvestment period of up to five years, usually, there is some flexibility to reinvest after that. When the CLO experiences an unscheduled principal loan repayment after the reinvestment period, the collateral manager may use that principal to invest in a new leveraged loan. Because leveraged loans have limited scheduled amortization (1% to 5%) per year, almost all the prepayments are unscheduled. The longer the CLO manager can keep the CLO close to fully invested, the better for the equity. That is because CLO equity benefits from higher leverage, and the CLO's upfront costs are amortized over a longer period. Also, if it weren't accretive to the equity to reinvest the unscheduled principal proceeds, the equity could simply call the CLO.

The CLO indenture will usually lightly restrict what leveraged loans can be bought with unscheduled principal prepayments. For example, newly purchased leveraged loans will probably need a final maturity shorter than the prepaid leveraged loan. Also, the new loan may need to have the same or higher rating and par balance. These terms are highly negotiated, and the more flexibility the indenture gives, the better for the CLO equity. Conversely, this potential extension of the CLO's life isn't favorable for the CLO's Note investors, as they usually prefer a shorter, defined life. If the CLO's cost of debt is below the rates currently available in the market, that's when the CLO equity investors will want the manager to extend the CLO as long as possible.

Some of the usual negotiated items are listed below and ranked by how effective they are at restricting the CLO's extension:

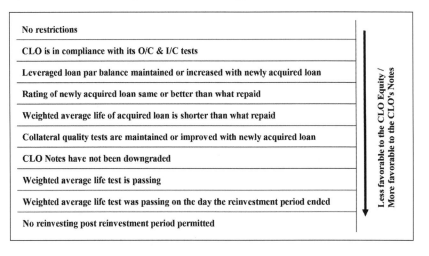

When modeling CLOs, a frequently used assumption is that after the reinvestment period ends, the CLO can reinvest 100% of unscheduled principal proceeds for three to six months. After that, the CLO's reinvestment restrictions will become hard to manage.

In markets where the Loan Index has traded down, it's much easier for a CLO to stay fully invested after the reinvestment period ends. That's because the leveraged loan prepayment rate will decline, as few borrowers would be eligible to refinance their debt at lower rates. Also, when the Loan Index declines, secondary leveraged loans are available at discounts to par value that may meet the required conditions of the CLO to continue reinvesting.

Below is an example of a CLO that has continued to reinvest over a year after the reinvestment period ended.

Reinvest End Date	15-Oct-21

Loan ID	Action	Date	Price	Principal Amount	Borrower
LX169970	Purchase	7-Nov-22	95.38	400,000	Hercules Achievement Holdings
LX169970	Purchase	7-Nov-22	95.50	600,000	Hercules Achievement Holdings
LX172008	Purchase	4-Nov-22	91.00	2,000,000	Amneal Pharmaceuticals
LX161694	Purchase	4-Nov-22	97.25	2,000,000	BWAY
LX175815	Purchase	4-Nov-22	96.00	3,000,000	Starfruit Finco B.V.
LX171161	Purchase	28-Oct-22	100.00	5,000,000	Formula One
LX169970	Purchase	28-Oct-22	93.00	111,874	Hercules Achievement Holdings

The CLO has an attractive cost of debt that could not be replicated at the end of 2022. If the CLO manager can buy loans that do not deteriorate the weighted average life test, the manager will continue reinvesting any unscheduled principal payments. Scheduled principal payments, the amortization agreed to in the leveraged loan documentation, cannot be reinvested and is instead used to repay the AAA Note. Shown below, the AAA Note has been deleveraging since the end of the reinvestment period.

Payment Date	Spread	Rating	Orig Balance	Curr Balance	Factor (% of tranche outstanding)	Principal Repay	Weighted Average Life	Weighted Average Life Limit
17-Oct-22	Libor + 1.08%	AAA	1,375,000,000	1,221,080,170	88.8%	30,457,626.22	4.02	4.00
15-Jul-22	Libor + 1.08%	AAA	1,375,000,000	1,251,537,796	91.0%	56,433,338.31	4.12	4.25
15-Apr-22	Libor + 1.08%	AAA	1,375,000,000	1,307,971,134	95.1%	18,490,178.77	4.12	4.25
18-Jan-22	Libor + 1.08%	AAA	1,375,000,000	1,326,461,313	96.5%	48,538,686.74	4.19	4.25
15-Oct-21	Libor + 1.08%	AAA	1,375,000,000	1,375,000,000	100.0%	0	4.25	4.50
15-Jul-21	Libor + 1.08%	AAA	1,375,000,000	1,375,000,000	100.0%	0	4.31	4.50
15-Apr-21	Libor + 1.08%	AAA	1,375,000,000	1,375,000,000	100.0%	0	4.41	4.50
15-Jan-21	Libor + 1.08%	AAA	1,375,000,000	1,375,000,000	100.0%	0	4.45	4.75
15-Oct-20	Libor + 1.08%	AAA	1,375,000,000	1,375,000,000	100.0%	0	4.53	4.75
15-Jul-20	Libor + 1.08%	AAA	1,375,000,000	1,375,000,000	100.0%	0	4.58	4.75
3-Mar-20	Libor + 1.08%	AAA	1,375,000,000	1,375,000,000	100.0%		4.65	5.00

Warehousing

7.1 Warehouse Overview

A CLO warehouse is used to acquire leveraged loans before the CLO forms. After the CLO's closing date, the CLO Notes begin accruing interest. Since a cash balance in a CLO does not earn an attractive yield for the equity, the manager will want to fully invest in leveraged loans as soon as possible. While the CLO manager can always identify leveraged loans to acquire in the secondary market, usually, the preference is to purchase leveraged loans slowly over time in the primary market. That allows the CLO manager to be as selective as possible. The investment banks that underwrite broadly syndicated loans often sell them so that a new issue purchase results in a lower price than buying the same loan in the secondary market. The goal of the warehouse is to deliver a portfolio of pre-purchased leveraged loans to the CLO, at a cost lower than if the leveraged loans were purchased in the secondary market. If the CLO's warehouse can save 0.5% on the cost of the leveraged loans, that could be worth 5% to the CLO's equity tranche, given the 10x embedded leverage in the CLO.

Usually, 60–70% of the CLO's leveraged loans are bought into the CLO warehouse. However, it's not a good idea to buy 100%. Let's say the interest costs for new CLO Notes begin to increase before the CLO's pricing date. That would be negative for CLO equity returns. In this case, having leveraged loans remaining to be purchased is probably positive, as these leveraged loans may be purchased at discounted levels. That's because the interest rates on leveraged loans and CLO Notes tend to move together. Said another way, the unbought loans are a natural hedge against potential increases in the cost of the CLO Notes.

The CLO warehouse is financed with ~20% equity, usually from the same investors that will purchase the CLO's equity. The remainder of the financing is debt from the CLO arranger. The warehouse debt financing is structured as a revolver, so the warehouse debt only funds when leveraged loans are purchased. Warehouse equity returns can be in the mid- to high-teens area. Because the warehouse is short-term in nature, it doesn't incur fees paid to the manager, underwriter, law firms, or rating agencies. The CLO will buy the loans in the warehouse at their initial cost so that the return to the CLO warehouse equity investor is the difference between the interest earned on the leveraged loans and the interest owed on the CLO warehouse debt.

Warehouse returns are increased during the month between CLO pricing and CLO closing. After pricing, the arranger knows the CLO will form, allowing for the warehouse leverage to increase from a loan-to-value of ~80% to ~90%, the same leverage level as the CLO.

The primary risk of investing in a CLO warehouse is that a newly bought leveraged loan defaults before the CLO closes. In that case, the leveraged loan will be ineligible for purchase into the CLO, and the warehouse equity will incur the loss. The probability of this happening is relatively low since the CLO warehouse is short-term, and the manager thoroughly diligences the leveraged loans before they are purchased.

A secondary risk to CLO warehouse investing is that the timing of the actual CLO formation is unknown. It depends on market conditions and how long it takes the CLO manager to purchase the portfolio of leveraged loans. Because the CLO's Notes are locked in place during the initial non-call period, the buyer of CLO equity will want the CLO to form when the CLO Note rates are favorable.

During the warehouse period, a hypothetical portfolio is created using the leveraged loans already bought ("ramped") in the warehouse with some assumptions from the manager about potential new loans to be purchased. This model portfolio is combined with projections for the CLO note costs, to project a return for the CLO equity. This kind of update happens many times during the warehouse, with the CLO equity investor ultimately deciding the best time to move forward.

Warehouse Update from a Ramping Warehouse

Loan Type	Par Amount	%	Bid Side Marks	WARF	Base Rate	Spread	Cost	Proceeds
Purchased LIBOR	118,136,403	29.5%	97.1%	2,668	LIBOR	3.46%	99.50%	117,545,721
Purchased SOFR	42,756,223	10.7%	97.2%	2,583	SOFR	3.82%	99.33%	42,469,756
Identified LIBOR	206,155,093	51.5%	97.0%	2,654	LIBOR	3.41%	98.61%	203,289,537
Identified SOFR	1,000,000	0.2%	97.4%	2,720	SOFR	3.30%	98.50%	985,000
To be identified	31,952,282	8.0%	99.3%	2,720	SOFR	3.40%	99.25%	31,712,640
Total	400,000,001	100.0%						396,002,654

7.2 Warehouse Returns Model

Below is a model for a warehouse opportunity. CLO arrangers rarely provide projection models for CLO warehouses because so many variables are highly market dependent. Thus, we build our projections and update them as the purchased loan portfolio begins to grow.

	Warehouse Pre Pricing CLO										Warehouse Post CLO Pricing		
Date	12/31/2022	1/14/2023	1/28/2023	2/11/2023	2/25/2023	3/11/2023	3/25/2023	4/8/2023	4/22/2023	5/6/2023	5/20/2023	6/3/2023	6/17/2023
Contributed Equity	10.00	10.00	14.00	18.00	22.00	26.00	30.00	34.00	38.00	42.00	42.00	42.00	42.00
Loans Owned		50.00	70.00	90.00	110.00	130.00	150.00	170.00	190.00	210.00	294.00	357.19	420.00
Leverage		5.00x	5.00x	5.00x	5.00x	5.00x	5.00x	5.00x	5.00x	5.00x	7.00x	8.50x	10.00x
Projected Spread on Loans		3.50%	3.50%	3.50%	3.50%	3.50%	3.50%	3.50%	3.50%	3.50%	3.50%	3.50%	3.50%
Libor		4.76%	4.82%	4.82%	4.82%	4.82%	4.97%	4.97%	5.07%	5.07%	5.09%	5.09%	5.11%
Total Loan Coupon		8.26%	8.32%	8.32%	8.32%	8.32%	8.47%	8.47%	8.57%	8.57%	8.59%	8.59%	8.61%
Debt from Investment Bank		40.00	56.00	72.00	88.00	104.00	120.00	136.00	152.00	168.00	252.00	315.19	378.00
Debt Spread		1.50%	1.50%	1.50%	1.50%	1.50%	1.50%	1.50%	1.50%	1.50%	1.50%	1.50%	1.50%
Interest Income		0.16	0.19	0.26	0.32	0.38	0.46	0.52	0.59	0.66	0.83	1.07	1.28
Debt Costs		(0.10)	(0.14)	(0.17)	(0.21)	(0.25)	(0.30)	(0.34)	(0.38)	(0.42)	(0.64)	(0.80)	(0.96)
Profit (Retained until the end)		0.06	0.06	0.08	0.11	0.13	0.16	0.18	0.21	0.23	0.19	0.28	0.32
Total Equity Cash Flows													
Warehouse Cumulative Profitability													2.01
Warehouse Principal Payments	(10.00)	-	(4.00)	(4.00)	(4.00)	(4.00)	(4.00)	(4.00)	(4.00)	(4.00)		-	42.00
Total Warehosue Cash Flows	(10.00)	-	(4.00)	(4.00)	(4.00)	(4.00)	(4.00)	(4.00)	(4.00)	(4.00)		-	44.01

Total Equity IRR 16.84%

Initially, $10 million of equity and $40 million of debt are used to acquire $50 million of loans. As additional loans are purchased, equity is called so that the equity amount is 20% of the cost of the leveraged loans. After the CLO has reached its pricing date, the leverage is increased to 90% loan-to-value. The CLO buys the loans at the price paid by the CLO warehouse, so the return to the CLO warehouse equity is the interest earned on the leveraged loans less the interest paid on the debt from the arranger. Often, the warehouse does not make any distributions to the equity until the day the CLO closes and the warehouse terminates. Retaining the warehouse's profitability is a positive for the warehouse debt provider, as it increases the collateral that backs their loan. Usually, the warehouse does not have any mark-to-market triggers; that means if the loans trade down in price, the warehouse continues its course. However, if there are downgrades to CCC/Caa or defaults in the warehouse, the equity investor will need to contribute more capital to the warehouse.

7.3 Print and Sprint CLO Formations

A lengthy CLO warehouse is certainly not a requirement to form a CLO. If leveraged loans are available at reasonable prices in the secondary market, the CLO equity investor may want to move directly ahead with the CLO; this is called a "print and sprint" CLO. The term "print" refers to printing trade tickets, which secure the CLO's funding. The term "sprint" refers to quickly buying leveraged loans. The faster the leveraged loans are bought, the less uninvested cash drags on equity cash flows.

Self-Healing

8.1 Loan Gains in Distressed Times

The CLO self-healing mechanism is a unique and favorable aspect of investing in CLOs. It's beneficial for both the CLO equity and BB Note investors. In recessionary periods, loss rates on the CLO's leveraged loans are expected to increase, potentially above the CLO equity investor's loan loss reserve. However, at the same time, some leveraged loans will be prepaid at par. When the loan prepayments come in, the CLO will purchase new leveraged loans. And in recessionary periods, leveraged loans should be available for sale at favorable prices.

In a typical year, one-third of the leveraged loans prepay at par. In recessionary years, the prepayment rate will be lower as businesses elect to keep their current financing in place rather than pay the higher market rate. But, even in markets like 2022, the estimated prepayment rate was around 15%. Each time a prepayment was received by the CLO, a new leveraged loan was bought with the proceeds at a discounted price. That builds in potential leveraged loan gains in the future.

In a normal market, many CLO analysts assume that when a leveraged loan prepays at par, a replacement leveraged loan will be purchased at a price of 99.0 or 99.5. However, in 2022 the Loan Index's average price was 95. The self-healing mechanism is powerful because many more leveraged loans prepay at par than default.

Loan Index vs. 99 Typical Reinvest Price — 2022

Source: Morningstar LSTA Leveraged Loan Index

Another way to think about self-healing is in yield terms. In a recessionary time, the CLO's operational costs do not change. The spread of the CLO's debt over LIBOR/SOFR and the management fees are fixed. However, as leveraged loans prepay, the CLO will purchase new leveraged loans with higher yields. If asset yields increase by 25 bps, for example, that can offset 25 bps of increased leveraged loan losses.

8.2 Self-Healing Forward Projections

In any recessionary market, a CLO analyst will want to quantify the potential magnitude of the self-healing mechanism as compared to potential increases in leveraged loan loss rates.

Several investment banks and rating agencies have projections for the leveraged loan market default rate in 2023. At the end of 2022, the average forecast was about 3.5%. Assuming the historical loan recovery rate of 65% shown in Section 2.10 above, that would imply 1.05% of leveraged loan losses: calculated as 3.5% default rate × (100% − 65% recovery rate). A potential 1.23% loss rate is significantly higher than the 60 bps loan loss reserve, but remember that this is only one year in the CLO's possible eight-year life.

At year-end 2022, the Loan Index was 92.44, a significant discount to par value of 100. The price decline of the Loan Index reflects higher required returns across all asset classes and the potential for higher defaults on leveraged loans.

In 2022, the leveraged loan prepayment rate was ~15%. For 2023, it might be marginally higher. Prepayments can be pushed into the future, but not indefinitely. Let's assume it's 20%.

When new leveraged loans are purchased into the CLO, unfortunately, they will probably not be bought at the price level of the Loan Index. That's because the Loan Index includes some stressed leveraged loans that wouldn't be appropriate for a CLO's portfolio given the CLO's leverage. With the Loan Index at 92.44, a CLO manager might find that leveraged loans bought at 96.00 have the credit metrics they require and that those leveraged loans will also help the CLO pass its many tests. In the case outlined above, the leveraged loan gains are 20% prepayment rate × 4% discount to par for the newly purchased loans = 80 bps.

Continuing with this example, expected losses are 1.23%, but there is already a loan loss reserve of 60 bps, which puts it down 63 bps. But the leveraged loan expected gains through the self-healing mechanism are 80 bps. The net result is positive 17 bps. In this example, the CLO equity is now likely to outperform initial expectations.

Of course, the scenario above is just one illustration of how loan losses and gains could play out. Below are some other potential outcomes.

Loan Loss Rate Per Annum

Column	A	B	C	D	E
Scenario	Default Rate on Loans	Recovery Rate on Defaulted Loans	Loss on Defaulted Loans (100% - Column B)	Loan Loss Rate (Column A x Column C)	Increase in Loss Rate vs. Base Case
Base Case	2.00%	70.00%	30.00%	0.60%	0.00%
Updated Case # 1	2.75%	65.00%	35.00%	0.96%	0.36%
Updated Case # 2	3.50%	65.00%	35.00%	1.23%	0.63%

Loan Gains

Column	A	B	C	D
Scenario	Prepayment Rate on Loans in CLO Portfolio	Price at which New Loans are Purchased	Loan Gains for CLO - Column A x (100% - Column B)	Increase in Loan Gains vs. Normal Market Environment
Normal Market Environment	25.00%	99.00%	0.25%	0.00%
Updated Case # 1	10.00%	94.00%	0.60%	0.35%
Updated Case # 2	15.00%	94.00%	0.90%	0.65%

Net Loan Gain / Loss

Column	A	B	C	D
Scenario	Expected Loss Rate	Increase in Loan Gains for CLO Portfolio vs. Normal Market Environment	Net Loss Rate - (Column A - Column B)	Net Loss Rate vs. Base Case 0.60% Loss Rate - (Column C - 0.60%)
Normal Market Environment	0.60%	0.00%	0.60%	0.00%
Updated Case # 1	0.96%	0.35%	0.61%	0.01%
Updated Case # 2	1.23%	0.65%	0.58%	-0.02%

While not offering a prediction of what leveraged loan losses/gains will be, the goal is to highlight for the reader the upside potential from CLO self-healing. When discussing historical CLO equity returns, the self-healing mechanism will play an essential role.

8.3 Self-Healing Historical Case Study

The CLO below saw an uptick in defaulted leveraged loans and Caa/CCC-rated leveraged loans during the COVID-19 downturn. After missing two equity distributions, the CLO leveraged loan portfolio had recovered to the point where the CLO equity distributions were turned back on. Buying discounted loans during the COVID-19 pandemic was a significant part of the recovery. This CLO recovered to the point where within a year of the peak COVID-19 downturn, the CLO refinanced portions of its Notes at lower costs—a fulsome recovery for the CLO equity investor.

| | Pre-pandemic | Pandemic low | Post-pandemic |
	2/20/2020	4/20/2020	4/21/2021
Market Price of CLO Equity (%)	52.5	37.6	54.5
Market Price of Loans (%)	95.4	85.3	97.4
Defaulted Loan %	0.7	2.6	1.2
Caa1/CCC+ or Less (%)	4.4	14.4	8.4
Weighted Average Spread (%)	3.5	3.5	3.4
CLO Cost of Debt (Spread over LIBOR) %	1.9	1.9	1.7
Net Spread %	1.5	1.5	1.7
Targeted Equity Return %	15.2	0.0	20.9

Flavors of CLOs

This book's focus is the most common type of CLO, the broadly syndicated loan CLO 2.0. Roughly 90% of CLO issuance is this type of CLO. But there are other CLOs in the market, as well as CLOs that are no longer issued.

9.1 CLO 1.0 and 2.0

A CLO 1.0 is a CLO issued prior to the Great Financial Crisis (GFC) of 2008–2009. On a buy-and-hold basis, the performance was strong across vintages from 2004 to 2007. These CLOs have all been repaid, but they are still an interesting historical relic to analyze. After the GFC, rating agencies decided that CLOs would need a greater equity percentage and the reinvestment period would be shorter. CLO Note investors also began requiring higher spreads. And the CLO equity investors obtained the ability to do refinancings and resets. From the perspective of the CLO Equity, it's hard to say who got the better end of the deal. From the standpoint of a BB Note investor, CLOs issued post-GFC are more favorable in terms of both risk and return.

CLO 1.0, Vintage 2007	CLO 2.0, Vintage 2022
Collateral Spread: ~L+250 Reinvest Period/Call Period: 7yrs./4yrs. Max CCC: 5-10% Collateral Type: BSL Issued pre-GFC	Collateral Spread: ~S+350 Reinvest Period/Call Period: 5yrs./2yrs. Max CCC: 7.5% Collateral Type: BSL Issued post-GFC
AAA Notes L+27 73% of cap stack	**AAA Notes** S+180 65% of cap stack
AA Notes L+50 6% of cap stack	**AA Notes** S+230 10% of cap stack
A Notes L+125 6% of cap stack	**A Notes** S+300 6% of cap stack
BBB Notes L+300 4% of cap stack	**BBB Notes** S+510 5% of cap stack
BB Notes L+600 2% of cap stack	**BB Notes** S+860 4% of cap stack
Equity Residual 9% of cap stack	**Equity** Residual 10% of cap stack

9.2 Static CLOs

A static CLO is a CLO that has no reinvestment period. Each time a leveraged loan is prepaid, the CLO will delever. An advantage of static CLOs is that the cost of debt is significantly lower than CLOs with a long reinvestment period. That's because the CLO's Notes investors view a quicker repayment as advantageous to getting repaid. From their perspective, the longer the reinvestment period, the more time loans have to default. Of course, there is no concept of self-healing in a static CLO.

Static CLOs generally make sense on two occasions. First, if the market for leveraged loans is trading at discounted levels, a static CLO can benefit from both the equity distributions from a favorable cost of debt plus the return from the CLO's leveraged loans, ultimately repaying at par. Second, static CLOs can make sense when the CLO equity investors have a short time period for the return of their invested capital.

Static CLO, Vintage 2022

Collateral Spread: ~L+350
Reinvest Period /Call Period: 0yrs./1yrs.
Max CCC: 7.5%
Collateral Type: BSL
Issued post-GFC
AAA Notes S+215 67% of cap stack
AA Notes L+305 12% of cap stack
A Notes L+400 6% of cap stack
BBB Notes L+600 5% of cap stack
BB Notes L+900 3% of cap stack
Equity Residual 7% of cap stack

9.3 Middle Market CLOs

Middle market CLOs represent approximately 10% of overall CLO issuance today and have some unique aspects that differentiate them from the broadly syndicated CLOs that are the focus of this book. Below are some of the salient differences between the two types of CLOs.

Criteria	Broadly Syndicated CLO	Middle Market CLO
Market Size	~$900 BN	~$100 BN
Leveraged Loans	Loans arranged by the largest US banks that also trade the loan	Loans arranged by a middle market investors who own the loan to maturity
Borrower Size	Companies with more than $400M of revenue	Companies with $200-400M of revenue
Number of borrowers	200-400	100-200
Financial Covenants	~20% of borrowers	~100% of borrowers
Spread on Leveraged Loans	LIBOR + ~3.5%	LIBOR + ~5.0%
AAA Note increased cost over Broadly Syndicated CLOs	N/A	~0.5%
CLO Leverage	10X Assets / Equity	7.5X Assets / Equity
Maximum CCC/Caa bucket	7.5%	17.5%
Historical Returns	Comparable to middle market CLOs	Comparable to broadly syndicated CLOs
Reinvestment after reinvestment period	Yes, for unscheduled principal prepays	Not permitted
CLO Equity liquidity in secondary market	Relatively liquid	Not liquid

Below is a detailed middle market structure compared to a broadly syndicated CLO.

Middle Market CLO, Vintage 2022	CLO 2.0, Vintage 2022
Collateral Spread: ~S+500 or higher Reinvest Period /Call Period: 4yrs./2yrs. Max CCC: 17.5% Collateral Type: Middle Market Loans	Collateral Spread: ~S+350 Reinvest Period/Call Period: 5yrs./2yrs. Max CCC: 7.5% Collateral Type: BSL Issued post-GFC
AAA Notes S+240 60% of cap stack	**AAA Notes** S+180 65% of cap stack
AA Notes S+350 8% of cap stack	**AA Notes** S+230 10% of cap stack
A Notes S+420 8% of cap stack	**A Notes** S+300 6% of cap stack
BBB Notes S+640 6% of cap stack	**BBB Notes** S+510 5% of cap stack
BB Notes S+1050 6% of cap stack	**BB Notes** S+860 4% of cap stack
Equity Residual 12% of cap stack	**Equity** Residual 10% of cap stack

A reason to invest in middle market CLO equity is that the projected returns are comparable to broadly syndicated CLO equity, but the volatility of those returns should be lower.

In broadly syndicated CLOs, the equity NAV will move around with the overall trading level of the Loan Index. Many factors that impact the Loan Index are related more towards technical rather than fundamental factors. For example, if loan mutual funds are getting redemptions, they need to sell leveraged loans, likely into a market where demand for leveraged loans is poor. The result can be a substantial move in the Loan Index and the broadly syndicated CLO equity NAVs. Middle market leveraged loans, by contrast, are not traded and do not experience price changes due to technical factors. As a result, the valuation of middle market CLO equity tends to track the fundamental performance of the underlying middle market loans. As illustrated in the chart below, the performance of middle market loans is significantly less volatile than that of broadly syndicated loans.

Date	Middle Market Returns	Broadly Syndicated Returns	Date	Middle Market Returns	Broadly Syndicated Returns
12/31/2022	2.1%	2.6%	12/31/2014	1.1%	-0.5%
9/30/2022	1.8%	1.3%	9/30/2014	2.4%	-0.5%
6/30/2022	0.5%	-4.5%	6/30/2014	2.8%	1.4%
3/31/2022	1.8%	-0.1%	3/31/2014	2.9%	1.2%
12/31/2021	2.3%	0.7%	12/31/2013	3.2%	1.7%
9/30/2021	2.7%	1.1%	9/30/2013	3.1%	1.2%
6/30/2021	4.0%	1.5%	6/30/2013	2.6%	0.2%
3/31/2021	3.2%	1.8%	3/31/2013	3.2%	2.1%
12/31/2020	3.7%	3.8%	12/31/2012	3.2%	1.4%
9/30/2020	3.5%	4.1%	9/30/2012	3.7%	3.4%
6/30/2020	3.3%	9.7%	6/30/2012	2.5%	0.7%
3/31/2020	-4.8%	-13.0%	3/31/2012	4.0%	3.8%
12/31/2019	1.9%	1.7%	12/31/2011	3.4%	2.9%
9/30/2019	1.8%	1.0%	9/30/2011	-0.2%	-3.9%
6/30/2019	2.3%	1.7%	6/30/2011	2.4%	0.2%
3/31/2019	2.8%	4.0%	3/31/2011	3.9%	2.4%
12/31/2018	0.8%	-3.5%	12/31/2010	4.4%	3.2%
9/30/2018	2.4%	1.8%	9/30/2010	3.4%	3.3%
6/30/2018	2.4%	0.7%	6/30/2010	3.8%	-1.3%
3/31/2018	2.2%	1.4%	3/31/2010	3.4%	4.6%
12/31/2017	2.0%	1.1%	12/31/2009	3.5%	3.8%
9/30/2017	2.0%	1.0%	9/30/2009	3.9%	10.5%
6/30/2017	2.0%	0.8%	6/30/2009	2.8%	20.4%
3/31/2017	2.4%	1.1%	3/31/2009	2.3%	9.8%
12/31/2016	2.6%	2.3%	12/31/2008	-6.7%	-22.9%
9/30/2016	3.1%	3.1%	9/30/2008	-1.1%	-7.0%
6/30/2016	3.6%	2.9%	6/30/2008	2.5%	4.9%
3/31/2016	1.5%	1.5%	3/31/2008	-1.1%	-5.7%
12/31/2015	-0.3%	-2.1%	12/31/2007	1.1%	-0.1%
9/30/2015	0.8%	-1.4%	9/30/2007	0.9%	-1.3%
6/30/2015	2.5%	0.7%	6/30/2007	4.1%	1.4%
3/31/2015	2.4%	2.1%			

Source: Morningstar LSTA Loan Index and Cliffwater Direct Lending Index

A second reason to favor middle market CLO equity is that middle market loans may experience fewer losses than the usual 60 bps CLO loan loss reserve. The reason is that middle market leveraged loans have covenants that put the lender quickly at the table if a borrower begins to underperform. In a workout situation, one or two lenders can usually drive towards a favorable outcome in middle-market leveraged loans. In broadly syndicated leveraged loans, dozens of lenders may get involved in the restructuring process, each costing time and resources. If a broadly syndicated borrower has a second lien loan, high yield bond, or preferred equity, the restructuring process becomes even more complex, with administrative costs eating into the first lien recovery. Additionally, the middle market loan documentation will be more protective of the borrower's collateral. Anecdotally, it's not hard to identify middle market CLO managers that have dramatically outperformed the 60 bps loan loss reserve.

One negative aspect of middle market CLO equity is that it's not very liquid. For broadly syndicated CLOs, any potential investor can see the public ratings of the underlying loans and the real-time loan prices. Middle market CLOs may have a trustee report with a recent price for the leveraged loans, but the price is more of a third-party appraisal than a real-time trading level. As a result, middle market CLO equity positions tend to be held to maturity. When the CLO begins to amortize, the CLO manager usually buys the leveraged loans at an appraised value and transfers the loans into another vehicle that is not amortizing.

The middle market CLO BB yield premium is 1% to 2% above broadly syndicated CLO BBs. And middle market BB Notes benefit from additional equity in the CLO. These securities are more liquid than middle market equity but less liquid than broadly syndicated BB Notes.

From a structural perspective, a middle market loan CLO has a four-year reinvestment period instead of the typical five years available for broadly syndicated CLOs. Additionally, in middle market CLOs, there is generally not a par flush which is advantageous for the CLO Notes. In middle market CLOs, when the reinvestment period ends, it's a hard stop. Reinvesting unscheduled principal payments is not an option.

In middle market CLO issuance, there isn't much overlap with broadly syndicated CLO managers.

Middle Market CLO Issuance — 2022

Rank	Manager	Size ($m)	New Issue ($m)	Reissue ($m)	Resets ($m)	Refis ($m)	Market Share
1	Golub	3,529	1,863	-	1,666	-	16.97%
2	Antares	2,321	1,259	-	1,062	-	11.16%
3	MidCap	1,897	962	-	935	-	9.13%
4	Blue Owl	1,681	1,144	-	536	-	8.08%
5	Cerberus	1,633	1,633	-	-	-	7.86%
6	Blackstone	1,589	1,589	-	-	-	7.64%
7	Monroe	1,311	959	-	352	-	6.31%
8	Fortress	746	746	-	-	-	3.59%
9	BlackRock	736	380	-	356	-	3.54%
10	First Eagle	724	724	-	-	-	3.48%

Source: Creditflux

Many of the above CLO managers do not sell CLO equity or BB Notes to third-party investors. Rather, the equity is retained by the manager and held in internal funds they manage.

9.4 Insurance Company Optimized CLOs

Insurance companies are sizeable investors up and down the various CLO tranches. Insurance companies are highly regulated regarding the ratings of the assets they buy. For example, an insurance company may want to own AA to BBB Notes. AAA Notes may not offer enough potential return for the insurance company, while the CLO equity and BB Notes would receive poor capital treatment from its regulator.

Insurance companies used to bundle purchases of various CLO Notes into a special purpose vehicle, which would have its own rating. This is referred to as a "combo note." The goal is to avoid unrated investments that would receive the poorest capital treatment, like CLO equity. For example, a combination of CLO BBB, BB, and equity might result in more favorable regulatory capital treatment than owning these notes individually.

Insurance company regulators are no longer favorable on combo notes, so the market has moved on to other structures, the goal of which is to maximize the sizes of the higher-rated CLO Notes and minimize the size of the equity tranche.

In the Insurance-Optimized structure shown below, a large X note rated AAA, can be considered an IOU from the equity. The BBB and BB tranches may have a turbo structure, which amortizes either tranche with proceeds that would have otherwise gone to the equity.

Insurance-Optimized CLO, Vintage 2022

Collateral Spread: ~S+500 or higher
Reinvest Period /Call Period: : 4yrs./2yrs.
Max CCC: 17.5%
Collateral Type: Middle Market Loans
BBB or BB notes may amortize

X Notes
S+205
5% of cap stack

AAA Notes
S+240
55% of cap stack

AA Notes
S+335
9% of cap stack

A Notes
S+410
9% of cap stack

BBB Notes
S+620
5% of cap stack

BB Notes
S+1050
5% of cap stack

Equity
Residual
12% of cap stack

9.5 Excess CCC/Caa CLOs

An excess CCC/Caa CLO owns a pool of broadly syndicated loans, but the CCC/Caa loan maximum bucket is set at 17.5% instead of the usual 7.5%. These CLOs attempt to capture an inefficiency in the leveraged loan market: traditional CLOs avoid CCC/Caa-rated leveraged loans because, in excess, they can disrupt payments to the equity. However, distressed debt investors may also avoid CCC/Caa-rated loans because they don't trade at prices low enough to entice them. The result is that many CCC/Caa-rated loans do not have a natural buyer. That's why the excess CCC/Caa CLO was created.

Excess CCC/Caa CLOs have a riskier leveraged loan portfolio with higher spread loans bought at a discount to par. Because the leveraged loan pool is riskier, the rating agencies require a higher % of CLO equity. Also, the cost of debt for the Excess CCC/Caa CLO will be higher, and the reinvestment period may be shorter. The challenge for these CLOs is that if market conditions are favorable, the CLO forms when there isn't a sufficient opportunity in CCC/Caa-rated assets. If the loan market is heading lower, and there is an opportunity in CCC/Caa-rated assets, it may be challenging to find CLO Note owners interested in participating in the deal.

Excess CCC CLO, Vintage 2021

Collateral Spread: ~L+425 or higher Reinvest Period /Call Period: 4yrs/2yrs Max CCC: 20.0% Collateral Type: Lower-Rated BSL Issued pre-Ukraine
AAA Notes L+195 55% of cap stack
AA Notes L+290 9% of cap stack
A Notes L+390 11% of cap stack
BBB Notes L+510 7% of cap stack
BB Notes L+755 4% of cap stack
Equity Residual 14% of cap stack

9.6 Balance Sheet CLOs

The CLOs I invest in have equity tranches owned by a third party, who is trying to earn favorable risk-adjusted returns. However, there are other CLOs created to add leverage to a loan portfolio that the CLO manager owns, like a Business Development Company (BDC). For example, many BDCs will borrow from a bank against their loan portfolio to increase the BDC's return on equity. And you can get a similar result by securitizing the loans in a CLO, where the BDC owns all the CLO's equity. These CLOs usually only sell down to the A Note, as restrictions on a BDC's total leverage may prevent the issuance of BBB or BB Notes.

MM Balance Sheet CLO, Vintage 2022

Collateral Spread: ~S+500 or higher
Reinvest Period /Call Period: 4yrs./2yrs.
Max CCC: 17.5%
Collateral Type: Middle Market Loans

AAA Notes
S+240
60% of cap stack

AA Notes
S+350
8% of cap stack

A Notes
S+420
8% of cap stack

Equity
S+640
18% of cap stack

CLO Modeling

10.1 Simplified CLO Model

One thing that makes investing in CLOs interesting is that each market participant uses different assumptions for their projection models. If someone says they recently bought CLO equity with a 14% IRR, it wouldn't be possible to know if they got a good or bad deal. Standardized modeling assumptions are what provide the answer.

Simplified CLO Model	
Inputs	
a. Forward LIBOR Average (Static)	4.00%
b. Leveraged Loan Spread over LIBOR	4.25%
c. Cost of Debt over LIBOR	-2.25%
d. CLO Manager Fees	-0.35%
e. Projected Loan Losses	-0.60%
Outputs	
Unlevered Return (a+b+d+e)	7.30%
Levered Return (b+c+d+e) x 9	9.45%
Total Return	**16.75%**

This model helps illustrate some basic CLO concepts, but it's not accurate enough for investing. The unlevered return of 7.30% is simply the return of owning leveraged loans in the CLO structure, assuming the CLO issued no Senior Notes. The levered return is the return increase from the leverage in the CLO.

In the above diagram, one thing to note is that each basis point of spread on the loans will equate to 10 bps of return for the CLO Equity, given the leverage in the vehicle. That means a CLO Equity investor must learn to care about the smallest changes in the CLO's economics. Colleagues have overheard me on the phone arguing about a basis point or two and asked me why I care about such a small amount. But yes, basis points are important, and they add up.

This simplified model is missing several key concepts:

- The underlying floating rate of LIBOR or SOFR will change over time.
- Leveraged loans in the CLO will prepay at par, and the CLO manager will reinvest those proceeds into new leveraged loans.
- Projected loan losses are not a current cost. Rather, defaulted leveraged loans stop paying interest into the CLO and result in a lower liquidation value for the CLO equity at the end of its life.
- There is no ability to make specific projections for unique loans in the CLO, like those trading at discounted levels.

10.2 Detailed CLO Model in Excel

Below is a more detailed financial model that addresses some of the deficiencies in the simplified CLO model.

Deal Assumptions

Initial Par (in thousands)	$ 500,000
Upfront Costs	0.60%
Reinvestment Period (year)	5
Leverage	10.0x
Annual Operating Expense	0.4%
Equity Purchase Price	95.0%

Example CLO Model from Year End 2021

Annual Inputs

Key Assumptions	12/31/2021	12/31/2022	12/31/2023	12/31/2024	12/31/2025	12/31/2026	12/31/2027	12/31/2028	12/31/2029
Asset Spread		3.50%	3.50%	3.50%	3.50%	3.50%	3.50%	3.50%	3.50%
Liability Spread		1.85%	1.85%	1.85%	1.85%	1.85%	1.85%	1.85%	1.85%
Loan Purchase Price		99.50%	99.50%	99.50%	99.50%	99.50%	99.50%	99.50%	99.50%
Prepayment Rate		35.00%	35.00%	35.00%	35.00%	35.00%	35.00%	35.00%	35.00%
Default Rate		0.00%	2.00%	2.00%	2.00%	2.00%	2.00%	2.00%	2.00%
Recovery Rate		70.00%	70.00%	70.00%	70.00%	70.00%	70.00%	70.00%	70.00%
LIBOR Projection	1.00%	2.90%	3.00%	2.85%	2.85%	2.85%	2.85%	2.85%	2.85%

Assets

	12/31/2021	12/31/2022	12/31/2023	12/31/2024	12/31/2025	12/31/2026	12/31/2027	12/31/2028	12/31/2029
Initial Par Value of Loans (in thousand	$ 500,000	$ 500,000	$ 500,879	$ 498,755	$ 496,640	$ 494,533	$ 492,436	$ 317,129	$ 204,231
Prepayments		(175,000)	(175,308)	(174,564)	(173,824)	(173,087)	(172,353)	(110,995)	(71,481)
Reinvests		175,879	176,189	175,441	174,697	173,956	-	-	-
Losses due to Defaults		-	(3,005)	(2,993)	(2,980)	(2,967)	(2,955)	(1,903)	(1,225)
Ending Par Value of Loans	$ 500,000	$ 500,879	$ 498,755	$ 496,640	$ 494,533	$ 492,436	$ 317,129	$ 204,231	$ 131,525

Income Statement

	12/31/2021	12/31/2022	12/31/2023	12/31/2024	12/31/2025	12/31/2026	12/31/2027	12/31/2028	12/31/2029
Income from Loans		$ 27,250	$ 32,278	$ 32,113	$ 31,604	$ 31,470	$ 31,336	$ 25,704	$ 16,553
Interest Expense		(17,100)	(21,621)	(21,479)	(21,042)	(20,943)	(20,844)	(16,675)	(9,902)
Management + Operating Expenses		(2,000)	(2,002)	(1,999)	(1,991)	(1,982)	(1,974)	(1,619)	(1,043)
Net Income		$ 8,150	$ 8,655	$ 8,635	$ 8,571	$ 8,545	$ 8,519	$ 7,410	$ 5,608

Equity Results

	12/31/2021	12/31/2022	12/31/2023	12/31/2024	12/31/2025	12/31/2026	12/31/2027	12/31/2028	12/31/2029
Equity Cash Flows	$ (47,500)	$ 8,150	$ 8,655	$ 8,635	$ 8,571	$ 8,545	$ 8,519	$ 7,410	$ 32,081
Cash on Cash Returns		17.2%	18.2%	18.2%	18.0%	18.0%	17.9%	15.6%	67.5%

Internal Rate of Return	13.9%

The CLO initially has $500 million of par loans. The upfront costs of 60 bps are paid to the CLO's arranger, lawyers, and rating agencies. The equity investor ultimately bears these expenses. A typical new-issue CLO has a five-year reinvestment period and 10.0x leverage, expressed as the par balance of CLO loans/equity amount. Annual operating expenses of 40 bps are almost entirely management fees.

The CLO's leveraged loans yield LIBOR + 3.50%, with LIBOR initially at 1.0%, for CLOs from the 2021 vintage. Since future LIBOR levels are unknown, the forward LIBOR curve is used to estimate future asset yields. Leveraged loans are purchased into the CLO at a price of 99.5, a slight discount to par. Each year 35% of the leveraged loans prepay at par. The collateral manager will buy new loans with the prepayment cash received at the same price and spread as the existing portfolio. The modeled default rate for the leveraged loans in the first year is zero. That's because the CLO manager recently bought all the loans; a newly purchased leveraged loan would rarely default in the first year. After that, loans are assumed to default at 2% per year at a 70% recovery (or 30% loss given default).

During the five-year reinvestment period, the par value of the CLO loan assets remains around $500 million. Loan losses reduce the par balance of leveraged loans, but reinvesting in discounted loans is a partial offset. After the five-year reinvestment period, the CLO begins to amortize. As leveraged loan prepayments come in, the CLO begins repaying its CLO Notes instead of investing into new leveraged loans. It's the AAA Note that gets repaid first. Then prepayments will begin to repay the AA Note, and so on. For simplicity, the breakout of the CLO Notes is not shown in the model. When the lowest-cost CLO Notes are repaid, the CLO's equity distributions will decline. In the model, the liquidation occurs in year seven, when the AAA Note is repaid.

Of course, the actual timing of the liquidation would depend on market conditions. Usually, CLO equity investors liquidate CLOs when the loans are trading near par to maximize their liquidation proceeds. A majority of the equity investors can decide to liquidate the deal.

The CLO's annual income is the par value of the CLO loan assets multiplied by LIBOR + 3.50%. The CLO's income is gradually declining initially because the LIBOR curve is downward sloping. Also, fewer leveraged loans (due to defaults) result in less income over time. CLOs have 10% initial equity, so the debt interest costs are high. But those costs also decline with LIBOR. Operating expenses are simply 40 bps × par balance of leveraged loans. There are no current expenses for credit losses, but as loans default, there is less interest income into the CLO and fewer loans to recover when the CLO is liquidated.

It's likely that some of the CLO Notes will be refinanced after the two-year non-call period. As the CLO moves through its reinvestment period, the risk that the CLO will default on its CLO Notes decreases. A future buyer of CLO Notes may, therefore, be willing to refinance the CLO's Notes at lower spreads even if overall market spreads have not declined. Perhaps the best scenario for the equity would be a refinancing in two years followed by a reset in five years. As elaborated below, the reset could extend the reinvestment period and materially increase the cash flows to the equity. However, in base case modeling, refinancings and resets are not included.

With the notable exception of static CLOs, the CLO manager will keep the CLO fully invested during its reinvestment period. The CLO's leveraged loans frequently prepay at par, leaving the CLO manager with cash to reinvest into new leveraged loans. Also, CLO managers may execute relative value trades where they sell a leveraged loan they expect to underperform.

Most CLO equity is sold at a discount to par. This can be thought of as the CLO arranger rebating some of its fee to the equity. The magnitude of the discount is highly negotiated because it's a key driver of equity returns. And the CLO arranger is very reluctant to give up part of its fee. For this CLO, a 95% purchase price is assumed. Cash-on-cash returns are quite high initially. But they decline over time, especially after year five, when the CLO begins to delever. When the CLO is liquidated, the equity recovers 53% from the liquidation of loans and an additional payment from the CLO's profitability. The CLO's equity tranche will rarely recover par, as its value is reduced due to projected losses on loans and the initial upfront costs of the CLO. The internal rate of return for the CLO equity is 13.9%, and all the CLO Notes are repaid at par.

10.3 CLO Modeling Using Third-Party Software

While it's certainly possible to model a CLO in Excel, most industry practitioners use software from Intex Solutions, Kanerai, or Bloomberg. Bloomberg has the advantage of being included in the Bloomberg terminal. These firms have already modeled in detail all the nuances of the CLO's payment waterfall, which can vary significantly from CLO to CLO. The nuances of diverting cash flows, if any of the CLO's O/C or I/C tests fail, would be a considerable increase in complexity for an Excel model. Additionally, with third-party software, it's possible to model projections for each underlying leveraged loan. Using third-party models, it's possible to get a good sense of the projected cash flows of any CLO quickly.

Third-party modeling software can significantly increase the number of input variables, with the expectation of more precise cash flow output. Many of the inputs will key off the different loan prices observed for the underlying leveraged loans. For example, if a leveraged loan is trading at a price below 90, the probability of default is elevated, and the likelihood of prepayment is reduced. For CLO equity and BB Note investors, the riskiest leveraged loans in the CLO are the most important to model correctly.

Below is a detailed list of material CLO modeling assumptions for normalized markets. In distressed markets, other input values may be chosen.

Modeling Item	Normal Market Input
Purchase Price for New Leveraged Loans	99.0%
Spread on Newly Purchased Leveraged Loans	3.5%
Annualized Default Rate for Loans Priced > 90	2.0%
Recovery Rate for First Lien Leveraged - Loans Lower of Market Price or	70.0%
Recovery Rate for Second Lien Leveraged Loans - Lower of Market Price or	25.0%
Annualized Default Rate for Loans < 90	100.0%
Time to Default for Loans Priced 80 to 90	2.0 years
Time to Default for Loans Priced 70 to 80	1.5 years
Time to Default for Loans Priced 60 to 70	1.0 years
Time to Default for Loans Priced 50 to 60	0.5 years
Time to Default for Loans Priced 50 to 60	0.0 years
Modeled Prepayment Rate for Leveraged Loans Priced > 90	30.0%
Modeled Prepayment Rate for Leveraged Loans Priced 80 to 90	15.0%
Modeled Prepayment Rate for Leveraged Loans Priced < 70	0.0%
Months after the CLO reinvestment period end for new leveraged loan buys	0.5 years
Collateral Liquidation Price at CLO's end - higher of weighted average loan price or	99.0%

Leveraged loans trading below 50 cents on the dollar might be assumed to default immediately and recover their current market value. A leveraged loan at 85 cents on the dollar is less risky, so a default in 24 months might be appropriate with a recovery of 85. In this case, the CLO benefits from two years of interest received and a higher recovery rate. And the table above details the default times and recoveries for prices in between. A leveraged loan trading below 90 is always modeled to default and recover its current market value; it's just a question of how much time passes before the default. Of course, this is just a modeling assumption, and many loans trading below 90 will ultimately repay at par. However, it's critical to differentiate a leveraged loan that is trading below 90 from one that is trading near par.

Loan prepayment rate is also a function of the leveraged loan price. Par loans might prepay at a 30% annualized rate. Leveraged loans trading in the 80s might have a 15% annual prepayment rate, while loans that trade lower than that may not prepay.

The weighted average price for leveraged loans trading above 90 must be calculated because that's a potential price to liquidate the CLO at the end of its life. During periods of market disruption, when the Loan Index trades down significantly, a floor liquidation price of 99 is often used. After all, the CLO's equity would not be incented to liquidate a CLO when the loans are trading at discounted levels.

Obviously, the real-world CLO performance will play out differently than the modeling assumptions above, but these are good simplifications of a complex reality.

10.4 Critical Nature of Correct CLO Equity Modeling

There must be no errors when modeling CLO equity. A CLO will produce a string of cash flows for an equity investor and nothing more—there is no par repayment when the CLO is called. In contrast, leveraged loans make a series of interest payments and then usually repay at par. Let's say, for example, there is an error in a model a financial analyst uses to project the cash flows of a leveraged loan borrower. Even with a modeling error, the mistake is unlikely to affect returns; the loan simply repays at par after several years. An initial loan-to-value of 50% provides significant downside protection. In CLO equity modeling, errors could result in IRRs materially different from what you initially expected.

At many financial firms, junior people run Excel models and the senior executives review them at a high level. In contrast, in

CLOs, the senior level investment professionals spend most of their days modeling CLOs because that's where all the action is! Using third-party models makes it straightforward to quickly analyze a new CLO and model many different return scenarios.

For CLO BB Notes, accurate modeling is important but less critical than for CLO equity. For example, without a detailed model, some basic CLO metrics could determine the likelihood that a BB Note would repay at par. Usually if the market value of the CLO's leveraged loans exceeds the sum of the AAA – BB Notes, then the BB Note is in decent shape.

For any CLO security that an arranger sells, the arranger would happily model out the cash flows using its internal models. Relying solely on these models is usually a mistake for the investor. Besides the assumptions detailed above, many other smaller assumptions can, in the aggregate, materially affect the CLO's projected equity returns.

Here is one example: The arranger might assume that when a CLO buys a new leveraged loan, the new leveraged loan will not default for 12 months. It's a reasonable assumption but not one that I use when modeling. By using my own models, I know that the assumptions the arranger is making are not influencing my results. That way, I can always compare CLOs on an apples-to-apples basis.

CLO Equity Investing

11.1 Sourcing CLO Equity

CLO equity can be bought in new issue CLOs (the primary market) or purchased from other market participants in CLOs that already exist (the secondary market).

In the primary market, the CLO equity investor becomes part of the process of bringing the CLO to life. Many investors gravitate towards the primary market because the primary market process has a nice feel to it. As the CLO comes together, the arranger, manager, and CLO equity investor work together to secure the best deal for equity investors. It's a team process; something is created.

In the secondary market, the only important item to discuss is the price you would be willing to pay. The trade is zero-sum; every incremental dollar saved on the price comes from the seller's pocket. There is no team process; instead, it's a lengthy negotiation on price with the seller.

In the primary market, CLO equity economics can be improved through negotiations. Some of the variables that determine the equity return will be fixed. For example, the purchase price and spread of the leveraged loan portfolio will not change. Similarly, as the CLO comes together, the cost of CLO Notes is also not usually a negotiated item from the equity investors' perspective. The arranger will negotiate the rate with the AAA Note, for example, but once that's fixed, it's no longer up for debate.

There are two material items that can be negotiated: the manager fee and the arranger fee. CLO manager fees are in the 30 to 50 bps range. The range is dictated by the manager's perceived skill and how well the CLO comes together. A typical arranger fee ranges from 20 to 40 bps of CLO assets (paid once upfront) and is a function of how challenging it's to sell the CLO equity.

Below are some of the pros and cons of buying in each market in normalized market conditions. The CLO equity investor must be informed about what is happening in both markets.

Primary CLO Equity

Pros:

- Long deals; potential to benefit from favorable reinvestments
- Potential to flush excess par on the first or second payment date
- Valuation is less NAV-dependent
- Newer loan pool; few loans trading sub-90
- CLO often comes together more favorably than initially modeled

Cons:

- Purchase price ~3.5 payments above NAV, can be expensive
- New deals have high debt costs
- First distribution often ~5 months from closing
- Initial portfolio is really hypothetical

Seasoned Secondary CLO Equity

Pros:

- Less expensive; often 1-3 payments above NAV
- Material upside if the CLO can be refinanced or reset
- Manager may have the ability to reinvest even after the reinvestment period ends
- If CLO is called, the proceeds may exceed the bid-side NAV commonly quoted
- If CLO is called, the timing of the call may be better than initially modeled

Cons:

- Reinvestment period shorter than a new issue deal
- NAV is larger driver of valuation
- More seasoned pool of loans
- If reset, new debt costs are higher

11.2 CLO Auction Process

In a Bids Wanted in Competition (BWIC) process, the owner of
CLO securities announces an intention to sell a CLO security on
a certain date. Investors submit their bids through an investment
bank, and the position is sold in an auction-like process. There
is no obligation on the part of the seller to trade. In fact, many
times the result of the auction is that no trade occurred. When the
position trades, the second-highest bid—the "cover bid"—is often
published to the market. This provides investors with valuable
market color. CLO equity does not trade through an exchange; as
a result, trades can be kept private.

An example of a BWIC process might look like this:

- The BWIC is announced a day or two ahead of time with
  a list of securities for sale. The BWIC will state a date and
  time on which bids are due.
- An investor combs through the list to determine which
  securities would be interesting to bid on and reaches out
  to a dealer to use for the bid. The dealer can provide deal
  documents such as the indenture, trustee reports, and the
  dealer's "NAV sheet" — its view on the fair market value
  of all the CLO's assets. These will help inform the price to
  bid on the security. Most investors will have a third-party
  pricing service for the leveraged loans in CLOs. However,
  double-checking the fair market values against a dealer's
  can be helpful.
- On the morning the BWIC is due, several dealers will put
  out "talk" on where they think the security is likely to trade.
  Once these are reviewed, the bid is finalized, and the dealer
  is asked if they can use the bid. If they have not received a

higher bid from another client, they will use the bid in the BWIC.

- Prior to the seller closing the auction process, another client may approach the dealer with a higher bid, in which case the dealer asks the investor to increase his bid. If the investor increases to a price above that of the new bidder, the dealer will continue with that bid in the auction.

- The time deadline for a BWIC is generally not strict, and late bids can still make it into the process. After the bid goes in, the investor waits to hear feedback from the dealer.

- Depending on the format of the auction process, the seller may simply sell the security to the highest bidder. Alternatively, the seller may begin negotiations with the top several bidders.

- In this process, the seller and the bidders remain anonymous. Only the dealer knows their identities.

The seller may decide not to trade the security at the end of the process, which is a frequent occurrence. If the security does trade, some color is often communicated to the market, the "cover bid" or second highest bid received in the auction. Putting out trade color is not a requirement of the seller. But an auction with no color provided will likely annoy other market participants.

11.3 Market Tracking

Investing in CLOs is a quantitative exercise. A best practice for an investor is to track all CLO opportunities in a format where comparison is easy. The tables below highlight some metrics to track when looking at CLOs to invest in. The first table is designed to answer the question, "What's the CLO like?" A later section focuses on returns and other market value analysis.

Deal	CLO Manager	Junior Most O/C Cushion	BB Par Sub	Deal Single 'B' Tranche	Weighted Average Spread (WAS)	First Call for CLO Debt (Yrs.)	Weighted Average Life (WAL) Test Cushion (Yrs)	Weighted Average Rating Factor (WARF)
CLO #1	Manager #1	5.31%	8.05%	0.0%	3.48%	0.94	3.68	2,777
CLO #2	Manager #2	4.64%	8.61%	0.0%	3.51%	0.42	3.32	2,763
CLO #3	Manager #3	3.73%	8.52%	0.0%	3.50%	0.00	1.55	2,620
CLO #4	Manager #4	4.13%	7.48%	0.0%	3.75%	0.00	0.32	2,759
CLO #5	Manager #5	2.17%	5.99%	0.0%	3.39%	0.00	0.83	2,854

Junior Most O/C Cushion

For the junior most O/C cushion, higher is certainly better. A CLO with 4% O/C cushion could theoretically have 13.3% of the leveraged loan portfolio default at a 70% recovery before the test fails, and equity cash flows get diverted [13.3% × (1 − 70%) = 4.0%]. Of course, a higher O/C test level will likely result in a higher purchase price.

BB Par Subordination

BB par subordination is the amount of equity in the CLO, assuming non-defaulted loans are worth par value. It usually starts at 8% or greater. Higher par sub indicates the CLO can be reset without issuing new equity. This metric is highly correlated with the junior most O/C test.

B Note Tranche

If the CLO issues a B Note, the CLO will be more levered than one that doesn't. The excess leverage is mildly accretive to base-case projected IRRs, but if CLO leveraged loans incur losses above the loan loss reserve, the increased leverage works against equity returns. Also, including the B Note can create another O/C test which could potentially divert cash flows from the equity.

Weighted Average Spread

The higher the weighted average spread on the leveraged loans, the higher the income into the CLO. However, higher spreads are also correlated with higher default risk on the underlying leveraged loans. CLOs with lower spread leveraged loans (LIBOR +3.25% to 3.50% area) are expected to have less volatility than CLOs with a higher weighted average portfolio spread.

First Call for CLO Debt

A majority of the CLO's equity investors have the right to call, refinance or reset the CLO's notes after a non-call period, generally two years for a new CLO with a five-year reinvestment period. Not being in the non-call period is better for the equity, regardless of whether the option is currently in the money. CLO equity investing requires accumulating options that may be valuable in the future without paying much for them today.

Weighted Average Life Test Cushion

Two items can determine the life of a CLO. The first is the end of the reinvestment period. For new CLOs today, the longest reinvestment period is five years. During that time, when leveraged loans prepay, the collateral manager will buy a new loan so that the CLO stays fully invested. However, in practice, the WAL test governs how long the CLO can stay fully invested, as unscheduled principal proceeds can be reinvested after the reinvestment period as long as new loan purchases do not worsen the WAL test.

Weighted Average Ratings Factor

This test converts Moody's ratings into an average numerical value, with a lower WARF indicating higher credit quality. A B2 loan rating is equivalent to a 2,700 WARF score.

Date	Deal	Diversity Score	Percent 2nd Lien	LIBOR AAA Spread	SOFR AAA Spread	Mgr. Fees	WA Bid Price for Loans	Loans Bid Sub 90
2/16/2023	CLO #1	78	0.62%	1.18%	N/A	0.25%	95.6%	13.2%
2/13/2023	CLO #2	96	3.10%	1.10%	N/A	0.32%	94.1%	19.2%
2/2/2023	CLO #3	92	0.60%	1.12%	N/A	0.35%	94.9%	14.6%
2/2/2023	CLO #4	N/A	1.76%	1.10%	N/A	0.50%	92.0%	24.0%
2/2/2023	CLO #5	102	0.97%	1.15%	N/A	0.50%	94.0%	15.2%

Diversity Score

The diversity score measures the number of obligors and their distributions in different industries. Higher diversity is beneficial, especially if the equity wants to refinance or reset the CLO in the future. Lower diversity loan portfolios can also be interesting if the manager is skilled in making higher-conviction investments.

Percent Second Lien

Each CLO has a basket for second lien loans. These loans offer 2–3% spread premiums to first lien loans but are higher risk, as they are second in line in a bankruptcy. A pool of 100% first lien loans are usually modeled with a recovery of 70% in the event of default, but if there are second liens in the CLO, a 30% recovery may be used. The result is usually a 68–70% modeled weighted average recovery value for the CLO's loan portfolio.

AAA Spread over LIBOR or SOFR

AAA Note spread is a proxy for the overall debt costs of the CLO, as this tranche finances ~65% of the CLO. Obviously, a lower spread is better for the equity, but the seller will want a higher price for the low funding cost of the CLO's Notes. The base rate of LIBOR or SOFR is determined by when the CLO was formed; any CLOs issued in 2022 and beyond use SOFR.

Manager Fees

CLO management fees can vary in the 30 to 50 bps range. The fee represents the manager's perceived skill and experience and the CLO's initial projected profitability when it was formed.

Weighted Average Price of Leveraged Loan Portfolio

When contemplating an investment in CLO securities, detailed information is needed on the underlying leveraged loans in the CLO. Thankfully, the CLO's monthly trustee reports provide almost all the necessary information. The one thing missing is the current market value of the underlying leveraged loans.

A few vendors provide prices for each CLO leveraged loan, including Bloomberg, IDC, and IHS Markit Partners. With real-time leveraged loan prices, analysts can calculate the total market value of all loans in a CLO. As discussed above, special attention is paid to loans trading under 90 cents on the dollar, as these loans are more likely to default than loans trading near par.

The weighted-average bid price of the leveraged loans will move around based on the specific performance of the leveraged loans and the trading level of the Loan Index. Usually, higher is better. However, loans trading above par may indicate that the loan will be refinanced at a lower spread in the future.

Loans with Price < 90

Theoretically speaking, the cheaper the loan, the higher the risk of default, holding other factors even. However, if all loans traded down by one point because the Loan Index moved lower, that probably wouldn't cause much concern. In fact, that may be a good thing, as the CLO reinvests in leveraged loans at a lower price in the future. On the other hand, if the weighted average price of the loans declined by a point because several loans traded from par to below 80, this would not be favorable, as the likelihood of default for those loans is elevated. Additionally, the below-90 price bucket is also moving with the overall level of the Loan Index.

Loan Index Trading Level

The Loan Index trading level provides the base level to evaluate the percentage of the portfolio trading below 90 and the weighted average price of the leveraged loans.

Would it be interesting to invest in a CLO with many loans trading below 90? Perhaps. The reason is that all these loans will be modeled as defaulting and recovering their current market value. The result is a lower purchase price for the equity, with upside if defaults do not materialize.

Date	Deal	Price Context	Implied Price	NAV adj. for X tranche	Liquidation NAV	Next Quarter Cash-on-Cash	Payments over NAV	IRR - 1.0% Default Rate	IRR - 2.0% Default Rate	IRR - 3.0% Default Rate
2/16/2023	CLO #1	71.33	71.3%	38.83%	38.83%	5.31%	7.6	20.71%	16.16%	9.53%
2/13/2023	CLO #2	59.50	59.5%	29.14%	23.38%	5.39%	>10	14.08%	9.94%	5.00%
2/2/2023	CLO #3	63.66	63.7%	39.54%	39.54%	4.85%	5.5	21.53%	17.49%	12.81%
2/2/2023	CLO #4	35.11	35.1%	-2.07%	-2.07%	5.90%	>10	17.95%	10.83%	2.56%
2/2/2023	CLO #5	18.03	18.0%	2.93%	2.93%	9.83%	>10	28.78%	19.09%	9.62%

Price Context and Implied Price

Price context is used to denote the trade color we receive. But the implied price column above indicates the price used to generate returns. The numbers can be different if a price can be negotiated lower than the initial offer. Also, the trade color may be quoted using industry-specific shorthand. For example, a BWIC that traded with a cover price of 75.5 might be described by the dealer as 75h or m75h (for 75-handle or mid-75-handle). The cover price from any BWICs for which color has been provided is used as the implied price in the tracking sheet for third-party transactions.

Net Asset Value Calculations

The liquidation value of the CLO is calculated in two ways. If there is no X Note, the NAV is calculated in the normal fashion. The second calculation subtracts the value of the X Note if there is one.

Next Quarter Cash-on-Cash

The next quarter cash-on-cash is the next projected equity payment divided by the purchase price. This is the CLO's initial yield.

Payments over NAV

Payments over NAV is the purchase price compared to the NAV in terms of future payments. Unless CLO equity is nearing the end of its life, the purchase price will usually be a substantial premium to NAV. The first CLO's price is 7.6 payments above NAV; that means in less than two years, you'll recover the premium to NAV. The NAV can be considered the floor value the equity tranche should be worth because the CLO could be liquidated at this value if the CLO's non-call period has expired. The high cash flows that the CLO equity tranche enjoys justify a purchase price above NAV. The higher the projected cash flows, the higher the premium to NAV. In the example above, paying 7.6 payments above NAV would make sense if the investor expected the NAV to increase.

IRR Scenarios 1–3% Default Rate

For projected IRRs, three cases are run, with default rates of 1%, 2%, and 3%. The leveraged loan recovery value is set at 70%.

The 1% default rate is an upside case, which is less of a focus than the other cases.

The 2% default rate is what most analysts optimize around. The 2% default rate has the standard leveraged loan loss reserve of 60 bps.

The 3% default rate is a downside case and a critical variable to consider. Shown above, the difference between the 2% default rate and the 3% default rate varies dramatically by deal. One of the key drivers of the difference is whether the CLO has extra leverage through a B Note. That extra leverage will be quite beneficial in the 1% default rate scenario but quite detrimental to returns in the 3% default rate scenario.

Additional IRR Scenarios

Other cases are also modeled, including potential refinancings and resets that aren't shown above. These cases are modeled based on current market conditions. Also frequently considered is the default rate required to result in a negative IRR.

Historical Equity Returns

Each CLO Equity tranche is ~$50 million in size and trades infrequently. And most trades are not publicly disclosed. The result is that accurate historical return information is difficult to find for the asset class.

12.1 IRRs for CLOs by Vintage

One way to track CLO equity returns is by the CLO's vintage or inception year. All the cash flows from the CLO can be aggregated using trustee reports. But we don't know the actual purchase prices for the CLO equity tranches, as that is not public information. For the data below, the assumed purchase price for the equity is 85, a good estimate consistent with industry practice.

IRRs for Terminated CLOs by Vintage

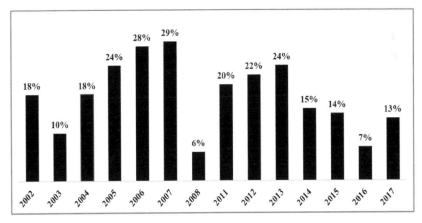

Source: Nomura CLO Research. 2009 and 2010 did not see CLOs issued. CLOs issued in 2018 and beyond are largely not terminated.

The chart above shows favorable historical returns for investors on a buy-and-hold basis. The IRRs are even more compelling when considering that when the CLO was formed, the purchase price was contributed upfront. The investor didn't have to sit in cash and wait for the capital to be called. It's also not a small allocation trade; an investor could have invested billions in the opportunity.

One surprising conclusion from the chart above is that the more exposure the CLO had to the GFC, the better the returns. An investor who bought CLO equity in the 2007 vintage likely targeted ~13% returns after factoring in the loan loss reserve. In 2008 and 2009, peak leveraged loan losses were closer to 4.0% (8% defaults × 50% recoveries). CLO equity, like other asset classes, was feeling the pain.

At the same time, the Loan Index hit an all-time low of 59. The CLOs were slowly getting repaid at par on some leveraged loans, and the CLO manager was buying new leveraged loans at discounted levels. Fortunately, many more leveraged loans were prepaid at par than defaulted. Over time, this substantially increased the CLO's profitability. In fact, the CLO's increased profitability from buying discounted leveraged loans exceeded the increased recessionary leveraged loan losses absorbed by the CLO. This is a case study of the self-healing mechanism discussed in Chapter 8 above.

For CLOs outstanding during the financial crisis, the average equity tranche missed two or three payments. Around 25% of equity tranches missed no payments at all—these were the CLOs managed by what are considered today's best managers. Their skill was both in picking leveraged loans that didn't suffer significant deterioration and understanding the rules of the CLO to maximize cash flows to the equity tranche. CLOs issued before the GFC had favorable debt costs. Many managers that outperformed worked hard to keep the CLO as fully invested as possible for as long as possible.

There isn't an index that shows where CLO Notes or equity tranches would have traded during the GFC. Equity and more junior debt tranches traded at very distressed levels, and investors who persevered were rewarded with solid returns. Many investors who sold at distressed levels during the GFC likely did not understand that CLOs could make up for the increased leveraged loan losses by buying discounted loans into the CLO.

CLOs issued shortly after the GFC also benefitted from buying loans at discounts to par value, as the leveraged loan market was still dislocated. Those CLOs benefitted as most of the discounted leveraged loan purchases ultimately repaid at par.

For CLOs issued 2015 - 2017, many had loan losses from the downturn in commodity prices in 2015/2016. Additionally, during this period, there was strong demand for leveraged loans, and many borrowers refinanced at lower rates, decreasing the CLO's income.

For CLO's issued in 2018 and later, most are still around, investing in leveraged loans and paying distributions to the equity tranche. For these CLOs, there isn't a realized return. However, these CLOs have distributed significant cash flows to investors, and have the possibility of future refinancings or resets.

12.2 Negative IRR CLO Equity

What's the probability of a negative return on a CLO equity investment? One investment bank researched all CLOs issued between 2002 and 2020 and found that fewer than 5% had negative returns. That surprises many people who erroneously lump CLOs in with CDOs that performed poorly during the GFC.

Negative CLO Equity Returns for Vintages 2002 - 2020

Source: Nomura CLO Research

To end up with a negative IRR, the CLO needs to perform poorly right out of the gate. That's because the equity tranche should quickly begin making substantial distributions. A negative CLO equity return would often be accompanied by both poor leveraged loan selection and an initial portfolio that didn't come together according to plan.

12.3 CLO Equity Index

The most common way investors think about returns is a market-weighted return index, like the S&P 500 Index. Because there aren't daily trading prices for CLO equity tranches, like stocks, a different method was used to calculate the return. It turns out that many of the owners of CLO equity are investment companies that are required to file the fair market value of their holdings quarterly with the SEC. If an equity tranche was marked at one price one quarter and another price the next, the return over the quarter can be measured. The quarterly distribution just needs to be added in. Using this method returns for roughly 25% of the CLO equity universe can be calculated in a database of quarterly returns that goes back to 2014. The result is the CLO Equity Index (cloequityindex.com).

One of the unfortunate drawbacks of the index is that it doesn't offer anything for real-time returns and can only be calculated on a time-lag basis as the investment companies file with the SEC within two to three months of quarter end. However, despite its drawbacks, it's still a valuable tool for showing historical returns for the asset class.

Date	Index Level	Quarterly Return	Yearly Return
30-Sep-14	100.00		
31-Dec-14	100.21	0.21%	
31-Mar-15	101.02	0.80%	
30-Jun-15	102.37	1.34%	
30-Sep-15	94.71	-7.48%	
31-Dec-15	83.92	-11.39%	-16.26%
31-Mar-16	83.57	-0.42%	
30-Jun-16	97.59	16.78%	
30-Sep-16	111.97	14.74%	
31-Dec-16	124.88	11.53%	48.81%
31-Mar-17	125.64	0.61%	
30-Jun-17	130.36	3.75%	
30-Sep-17	128.54	-1.39%	
31-Dec-17	134.11	4.33%	7.39%
31-Mar-18	138.53	3.29%	
30-Jun-18	139.59	0.77%	
30-Sep-18	142.52	2.10%	
31-Dec-18	121.72	-14.59%	-9.24%
31-Mar-19	133.55	9.72%	
30-Jun-19	133.13	-0.31%	
30-Sep-19	119.74	-10.06%	
31-Dec-19	121.00	1.05%	-0.59%
31-Mar-20	84.21	-30.41%	
30-Jun-20	90.61	7.60%	
30-Sep-20	102.83	13.49%	
31-Dec-20	132.51	29.89%	9.51%
31-Mar-21	144.49	9.04%	
30-Jun-21	156.87	8.57%	
30-Sep-21	169.09	7.79%	
31-Dec-21	172.15	1.81%	29.91%
31-Mar-22	168.63	-2.04%	
30-Jun-22	147.58	-12.49%	
30-Sep-22	152.05	3.03%	
31-Dec-22	152.18	0.09%	-11.60%

CLO Equity Index Total Return Level

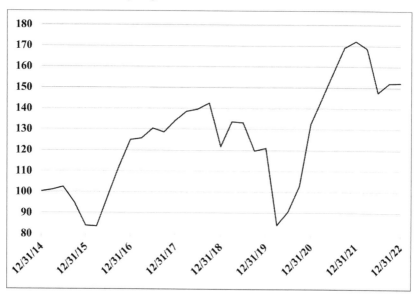

CLO Equity Index Summary Statistics

One-Year Return	Three-Year Return Annualized	Five-Year Return Annualized	Annual Return Since inception on 9/30/2014	Maximim Quarterly Drawdown	Maximim Quarterly Drawdown Period	Standard Deviation of Returns
-11.6%	7.9%	2.6%	5.2%	-30.4%	1Q2020	21.2%

From the Index's inception in September 2014, the Index returned 5.2%, a surprisingly low result given the merits of CLO equity discussed in this book. There are a few factors that weigh heavily on the Index returns:

- We chose 2014 as the starting point because that's when we had a sufficient data set for our results to be generalizable. By excluding 2010 to 2013, we lost years that would have been significantly accretive to historical returns.

- The 2014 to 2022 period saw four economic downturns: the oil and gas commodity price declines in 2015/2016, a taper tantrum in 2018, a COVID-19 sell-off in 2020, and the Federal Reserve interest rate hiking of 2022. The COVID-19 peak drawdown resulted in an index decline of 30.4%.

- In 2022, interest rates increased substantially, and most asset classes traded down. However, leveraged loan default rates did not increase materially. If the refinancing and reset market opens up, index returns have the potential to increase substantially.

- The returns above exclude any returns from investments in CLO warehouses, which are often in the high teens. Warehouses are private transactions that aren't reported in the sample set.

12.4 CLO Equity Highest Returns

In the list of best-returning CLOs, there are a few that are outstanding for only a year. For these CLOs, the manager locked in the cost of debt and was able to buy loans in a dislocated market. As the loans recovered in value, the CLO equity investors decided to take their gains and liquidate the CLO.

Rank	Deal	Closed	Redeemed	Manager	IRR (%)
1	Jackson Square CLO	2009	2009	Blackstone (formerly GSO)	154.7%
2	RR 10	2020	2021	Apollo Global Management (Redding Ridge)	93.7%
3	SCFF 1	2020	2021	Apollo Global Management (Redding Ridge)	62.8%
4	Stratus 2020-1	2020	2021	Blackstone (formerly GSO)	62.3%
5	RR 11	2020	2021	Apollo Global Management (Redding Ridge)	54.4%
6	Gemini Fund	2002	2014	GSC Partners/Black Diamond	49.6%
7	RR 9	2020	2021	Apollo Global Management (Redding Ridge)	48.4%
8	Restoration Funding	2002	2007	Highland Capital Management	39.5%
9	Rad CLO VIII	2020	2021	Irradiant Partners	35.8%
10	Copper River	2007	2015	Guggenheim Investments	34.0%
11	Dryden High Yield CDO -2001-1	2001	2007	PGIM	31.0%
12	Madison Park Funding V	2007	2017	Credit Suisse Asset Management	31.0%
13	1888 Fund	2002	2013	Guggenheim Investments	30.8%
14	Apidos Cinco	2007	2016	Apidos/CVC Credit Partners	30.6%
15	Golub Capital Partners 2007-1	2007	2015	Golub Capital	30.6%
16	KKR Financial CLO 2007-A	2007	2014	KKR	30.1%
17	ALM VII	2012	2021	Apollo Global Management (Redding Ridge)	29.5%
18	Madison Park Funding IV	2007	2017	Credit Suisse Asset Management	29.1%
19	Stone Tower CDO	2003	2005	Stone Tower/Apollo	28.9%
20	Madison Park Funding VI	2007	2017	Credit Suisse Asset Management	28.6%

Source: Creditflux

CLO BB Notes

13.1 CLO BB Basics

The CLO BB Note investor buys a debt instrument that targets equity-like returns. All the leveraged loans in the CLO are security for the BB Note, but Notes with higher priority have the more senior claim on the CLO's assets.

The CLO BB Note is usually the junior-most note that finances the CLO. It benefits from the initial equity in the CLO, which will absorb the first losses on the portfolio. It also benefits from CLO structural protections that divert cash flows from the equity to the benefit of the noteholders if the risk in the underlying leveraged loans increases substantially. The CLO BB Note pays an interest rate of LIBOR or SOFR plus a spread. At the end of 2022, LIBOR was 4.75%, and the average spread over LIBOR was 9.80%, for a total rate of 14.55%.

Investing in CLO BBs carries a different set of considerations and a different risk/return profile than equity, but the fundamentals are largely the same. The first dollar of principal leveraged loan losses impacts the returns of CLO equity, but BB Notes are money-good until every dollar of equity has been lost in the transaction. Additionally, in stressed scenarios, the cash flow that would normally be paid to the equity gets redirected to buy additional leveraged loans or pay down debt more senior than the BB Note.

A typical broadly syndicated loan CLO BB can withstand annual defaults of 7%. CLO BBs generally have a lower projected return than CLO equity because they are senior in the capital structure.

CLO Equity	CLO BBs
First loss on leveraged loan defaults in the CLO	Equity acts as a buffer against losses
Variable cash flows based on a number of factors	Cash flow based on base rate + fixed spread
Higher risk / higher return	Lower risk / lower returns
Has right to call/reset deal after non-call period	No rights to dictate how long CLO is outstanding
Less liquid in secondary trading	More liquid in secondary trading

All CLO Notes have the same fixed maturity, usually 12 years from the CLO's inception. The maturity date is set so that all the CLO's leveraged loans will be repaid by that date. For example, a CLO manager could buy a new leveraged loan with a six-year maturity at the end of a five-year reinvestment period. That leveraged loan should be repaid sooner than 11 years from the CLO's inception date. That would provide one additional year of cushion to ensure all the leveraged loans are repaid by the CLO's maturity date.

However, in almost all cases, the CLO BB Note will be repaid much sooner than the CLO's maturity. That's because the CLO's equity investor will want to keep the CLO fully invested. Having an extended period in which the CLO delevers after the reinvestment period produces non-optimized cash flow for the CLO equity. If a CLO starts with a two-year non-call period, we know the BB Note will be outstanding for at least that long. As the CLO gets closer to the end of its reinvestment period, the CLO equity investor may want to do a reset, which would extend the CLO's reinvestment period. If that happens, the CLO BB would be repaid at par. After the end of the non-call period, the CLO BB could also be refinanced at a lower rate, resulting in a par repayment for the CLO BB investor.

There are two reasons a CLO BB might be outstanding two or three years after the reinvestment period ends:

(1) The CLO's cost of debt is below current market levels, and the CLO equity investor would rather keep the low financing cost even though the CLO is deleveraging.

(2) The CLO has materially underperformed. The CLO equity investor cannot call the deal unless all the CLO's Notes can be repaid at par. If the equity NAV is negative, the CLO will naturally delever over time after the reinvestment period. The CLO equity investor would not be incented to call a deal unless there is a material recovery in the equity NAV. Otherwise, he will wait and hope the leveraged loans increase in value.

There are three sources of risk for the CLO Note investor:

(1) Mark-to-market unrealized depreciation

(2) Actual risk of default

(3) Rating agency downgrade

Some market participants consider CLO equity to be less risky than BB Notes. I disagree, but their rationale is that CLO equity cash flows are front-end loaded, with an average duration of three years. The holder of a BB Note may have to wait eight years or more before receiving any principal repayment. In that time, many things could go wrong.

13.2 CLO BB Returns

From 2012 through 2022, CLO BB Notes returned 7.1% annually. It's a solid return considering how low interest rates were during this time. From 2012 to 2022, there were many downturns on the

CLO's levered loans, but none were severe enough to materially impact the CLO's BB Notes.

Future BB Note returns should be higher, as LIBOR and SOFR increased substantially in 2022, and most CLO BB Notes were also trading below par value.

CLO BB Note Annual Returns

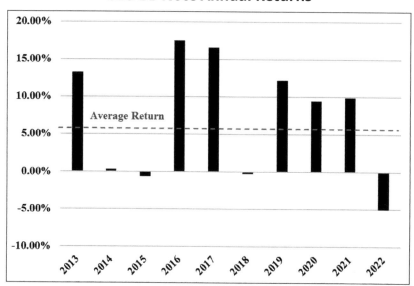

Source: Palmer Square CLO Indices

13.3 CLO BB Structural Features

The CLO's initial equity absorbs the first losses on the CLO's leveraged loan portfolio. But there is a significant credit enhancement for the CLO's Note investors in the potential to divert equity tranche payments to benefit the CLO's Notes. Before a CLO makes an equity distribution, the CLO needs to be passing its O/C and I/C tests. The equity distribution will not be made if excess defaulted leveraged loans or CCC/Caa-rated loans are in the portfolio. The equity cash flow is diverted to either buy more leveraged loans or repay AAA Notes, depending on how poorly the CLO performs against its tests.

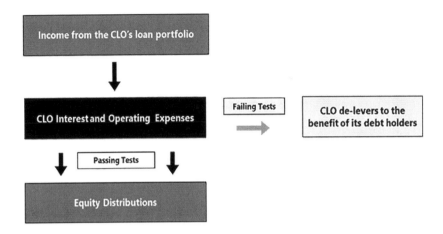

Below is an example of how this worked for one middle market CLO. During the COVID-19 period, the CLO saw a sharp increase in defaults and CCC/Caa-rated loans. In July and October of 2020, cash flow was diverted from the equity, thereby increasing the credit quality of the CLO BB and other CLO Notes.

Middle Market CLO — Vintage 2015

CLO Payment Date	CCC % of Loans	Defaulted % of Loan	Equity Distribution	Additional Loan Collateral Purchased	CLO AAA Early Debt Repayment
7/29/2022	11.47%	2.19%	2,640,665		0
4/29/2022	12.00%	0.86%	2,829,972		0
1/29/2022	13.61%	0.00%	3,080,771		0
10/29/2021	14.86%	0.00%	2,996,884		0
7/29/2021	15.21%	0.00%	3,187,224		0
4/29/2021	17.84%	0.95%	2,908,345		0
1/29/2021	16.59%	0.95%	2,720,285		0
10/29/2020	16.52%	5.10%	1,127,641	1,420,267	0
7/29/2020	18.89%	3.90%	0		2,080,871
4/29/2020	16.45%	2.96%	2,377,206		0
1/29/2020	6.86%	1.59%	2,439,131		0

The CLO above is from the 2015 vintage. That means before the COVID-19 downturn, the CLO had five years of loan losses in the portfolio. That put it in a worse position to endure a downturn than a newly issued CLO. And a CLO equity tranche five years into its life has often recouped its full investment.

The initial CLO equity plus the potential to divert equity distributions in a downside scenario make it quite difficult for a BB Note to default. Typical modeling indicates a default rate of 7% would be needed throughout the entire eight-year life of the CLO for the BB Note to default, assuming the CLO began its life with 8% equity and assuming defaulted loans recover 70% of par value. During the GFC, leveraged loan defaults increased to 8.0% but returned to a more normalized level of 2% soon afterwards. Defaults were also elevated during the COVID-19 pandemic.

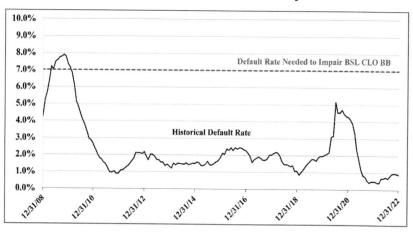

BB Note Default Resiliency

Source: Historical default rate from JP Morgan Research. BB Note results correspond to broadly syndicated CLOs with a five-year reinvestment period. The chart assumes a loan recovery rate of 70% and a pre-payment rate of 25%.

The CLO self-healing mechanism is also valuable to the CLO Note investors. In periods of financial stress, the leveraged loan prepayment rate will fall. However, new leveraged loans may be purchased at a significant discount to par value. If the discounted loans pay off at par, as expected, the result is additional collateral for the CLO Note investors.

13.4 CLO BB Note Default Rate

The historical default rate for CLO Notes by tranches is shown below.

CLO Note Default Rate

Ratings	Total Rated	Total Defaulted	Annualized Default Rate
AAA	5,085	0	0.00%
AA	3,480	1	0.01%
A	3,162	5	0.03%
BBB	2,939	9	0.06%
BB	2,323	29	0.25%
B	412	12	0.58%

Source: S&P Global Ratings, April 2023, assumes a 5-year average life

No CLO AAAs have defaulted, but as you move to CLO Notes less senior, the number of defaults picks up. But it's still quite small. Though the B Note is riskier than the BB Note, fewer B Notes are issued, which explains the fewer defaults in that category.

Since 29 out of 2,323 BB Notes defaulted, the cumulative default rate is 1.25%. However, analysts usually talk about default rates in annual terms. Assuming the average BB Note is outstanding for five years, the annual default rate is 0.25%.

Recovery rates improve with seniority. For the BB tranche, the average recovery is 43%.

CLO Recovery Rates

Original Rating	Average Recovery
Baa	65%
Ba	43%
B	30%

Source: Moody's Investor Service, 1993-2001

The default rate for CLO BB notes since 1994 is one-tenth that of high yield bonds and levered loans. For any particular loan, the CLO's collateral manager may pick one that goes bad. However, the number of poor picks necessary to result in a CLO BB default has been rare. Also, surprisingly, the BB Note has a higher spread than the loan index.

Security Default Rates

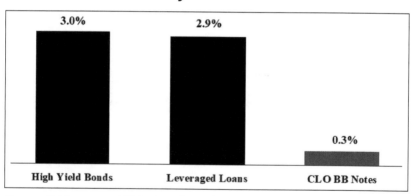

Source: JP Morgan and S&P; data through March 2023

13.5 CLO BB Note Investment Strategies

The most basic investment strategy in CLO BB Notes is to make investments with the highest potential return while minimizing the risk that the investment defaults. BB Notes are usually purchased below par value. The shorter the BB Note is outstanding, the higher the return. Understanding the likely life of the CLO BB Note is, therefore, key to success in investing in these securities. While CLO equity can offer projected returns of mid to high teens at times, the BB Note return profile is capped by a par payout.

Where the CLO Equity holders can call the CLO, refinance the debt or reset the transaction, the BB Notes (and other debt tranches) are "along for the ride." In markets where CLO Note costs are increasing, the equity holders are unlikely to refinance the CLO. This is negative for the BB Note investors, who own a lower-yielding asset than what they could acquire in the current market. In a scenario where CLO's cost of financing is decreasing, the equity is likely to refinance CLOs outside of their non-call period, resulting in the BB Note getting repaid at par.

Many of the metrics used to evaluate investments in CLO BB Notes mirror those used to evaluate the equity tranche. Failing collateral quality tests may not impact returns of the CLO BB as directly as the equity tranche but is still indicative of the overall health and quality of the underlying assets of the CLO. If a CLO fails its BB O/C test, distributions to the equity will be shut off, but this will not necessarily impact cash flows to the BB Notes. This scenario may actually help to improve the BB Notes' credit profile, as cash that otherwise would have been distributed to the equity will be used to pay down debt for the most senior CLO Note. However, the O/C test will only fail if significant CCC/Caa-rated leveraged loans or defaults are in the portfolio. Of course, the BB Note investors would prefer a higher-quality collateral pool.

Other CLO tranches have O/C tests set with more cushion than the BB Note test. If the BBB O/C test fails, interest payments to the BB Note will be diverted to pay down the AAA Notes. In this case, the CLO BB Note interest will be Paid-In-Kind or "PIK." This is a rare occurrence, and only 14% of CLO BBs PIK'd during the COVID-19 downturn, all of which were subsequently cured (the BB Note eventually received all interest due). The interest PIK is paid in cash when/if the BBB O/C test passes.

13.6 Par Subordination

The par sub of the CLO BB is the amount of equity supporting the BB Note, assuming the underlying leveraged loans are all worth par (unless they have defaulted). This number typically starts at 8% for broadly syndicated CLOs.

Since all the non-defaulted leveraged loans in the CLO are counted at par in this calculation, par sub does not move around with market price fluctuations in the underlying leveraged loans in the CLO.

A drop in par sub, or "par burn," can occur when levered loans default or if the CLO manager trades out of levered loans below the cost at which they were initially purchased. The manager may opt to do this if it believes the leveraged loan will continue to deteriorate or if it's looking to reduce CCC/Caa-rated loans in consideration of O/C tests.

An increase in par sub, or "par build," occurs when the manager buys performing loans below par. Since the par sub calculation counts any non-defaulted loans at par, such a purchase is immediately accretive to the par subordination of the deal. Another way that par build can occur is if O/C or I/C tests fail and the cash flow is used to buy more leveraged loans or pay down the AAA Note.

13.7 Market Value Over Collateralization

The Market Value Over Collateralization (MVOC) is the percentage by which the BB Note and all notes senior to it would be covered if the CLO were liquidated at the market price of the CLO's assets.

Since the current market value of the leveraged loans in the CLO fluctuates daily, this number will also fluctuate daily.

For CLO BB investors, this number becomes increasingly important as the CLO approaches the end of its reinvestment period. After the reinvestment period ends, the CLO manager will have significantly less flexibility to offset defaults through trading gains, and the CLO is closer to when a liquidation may occur.

If the CLO's leveraged loans decline in value, the MVOC can approach or drop below 100%. This is viewed negatively by the market, and the value of the CLO BB will decline in the secondary market. Even though it may not be years until the CLO is liquidated or the BB Note is repaid, investors do not like being in a debt security that is not fully covered in a liquidation.

Below is a comparison of one CLO BB's par sub and MVOC alongside the Loan Index at two separate time points, illustrating how the MVOC moves more dynamically with the loan market while the par sub reacts only to actual credit events in the CLO.

1/22/2022	10/22/2022
Par Subordination: 6.54%	Par Subordination: 6.41%
MVOC: 105.32%	MVOC: 99.08%
Loan Index: 99.04%	Loan Index: 92.21%

The Loan Index traded from 99.04 to 92.21 between these two periods, with MVOC moving commensurately from 105.32% down to 99.08%. However, since there were no new defaults in the portfolio, the par sub remained relatively constant at 6.41% vs. 6.54% before the loan market declined.

For an investor in BB Notes, the MVOC is more important than par sub because the fair market value of the leveraged loans is obviously a variable that can't be ignored.

13.8 Discount Margin

Most trading in BB Notes is done quoting the Discount Margin, or DM. The Discount Margin represents the all-in spread over a base rate (LIBOR or SOFR) that the CLO BB will return, assuming the CLO is not called early. DM comprises both the floating-rate coupon of the BB Note and any discount that the note was purchased at, amortized over its remaining life. Industry-standard assumptions for calculating a DM include a 20% annual leveraged loan repayment rate along with a 2% loan default rate and a 70% loan recovery. Under this scenario, the CLO BB Note is usually repaid within five years of the reinvestment period ending.

Some additional notes on Discount Margin:

- If a BB Note is bought at par, the discount margin will equal the spread.
- The shorter the expected life of the CLO, the more a discount in price will increase the DM (the discount is being amortized over a shorter period).
- The DM assumes that a BB Note will remain outstanding through the amortization of the CLO. However, this is rarely the case. CLOs will usually get refinanced or reset much sooner. In a scenario where the BB Note gets taken out earlier, one with a DM comprised of a higher discount and lower coupon will result in a higher IRR for the

investor than a BB Note with the same DM, but with a higher coupon and a lower discount.

- When new CLOs are issued, the arranger will negotiate DM and dollar price with investors. The coupon will then be determined based on the negotiated levels.
- From the perspective of the CLO equity, when new CLOs are formed, the preference is for the BB Note to be sold at par. In that case, any BB Note early prepayments will not result in a high return for the CLO BB Note. Also, when CLO BB Notes are sold at a discount, there needs to be additional equity contributed to the CLO to make up for the shortfall in proceeds.

The relationship between the price of the CLO BB Note and the DM is shown in the charts below. The lower the purchase price, the higher the DM. The graph below is highly correlated to the Loan Index. The big drops occurred during the commodity price declines in 2015/2016, the start of the COVID pandemic of 2020, and the potential for a recession in 2022.

Historical CLO BB Prices

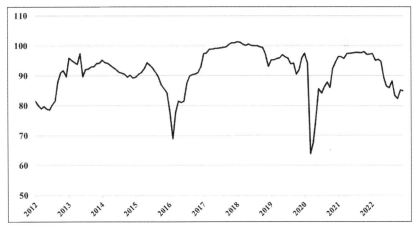

Source: Palmer Square CLO Index

Historical CLO BB Discount Margins

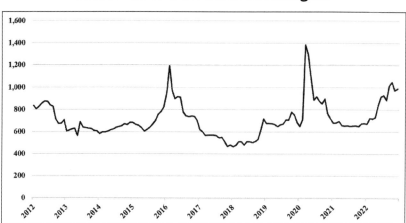

Source: Palmer Square CLO Index

13.9 BB Note Trading

Like CLO Equity, CLO BB Notes trade on the secondary market via BWICs and directly with banks' trading desks. CLO BBs are significantly more liquid than CLO Equity. It's partially because the return profile for CLO BB Notes is simpler to model. After all, the CLO equity absorbs the first losses on the leveraged loan portfolio.

Tracking the CLO BB market is similar to monitoring CLO equity, but there are a few BB-specific metrics:

- Discount Margin: As discussed above, DM is the most commonly referenced return metric used when trading BBs.
- MVOC: This is an important metric for BB trading (discussed above).
- Original Tranche Thickness: This represents the percentage of the CLO that the BB Note comprises. If a BB Note becomes impaired and is a thin percentage of the capital

structure, its recovery can quickly go to zero if further leveraged loan deterioration occurs. A thicker BB Note has a better chance of a positive recovery when it becomes impaired.

- Single B % of Capital Structure: Investing in BBs where there is a B Note in the capital structure adds further complexity. That's because for a CLO to be called, the CLO must be able to fully cover all of the tranches of outstanding debt with proceeds from the sale of the levered loans. While the B Note is subordinated to the BB Note, its existence results in a higher required weighted average leveraged loan price for a call to be possible.

- End of RP & Years since RP End: tracks when the CLO's reinvestment period ends and calculates how many years it has been since the end of the RP (a negative number if it has not occurred yet). Unlike CLO Equity, it's beneficial for BB Note investors to have a shorter duration on their investment. The faster a BB Note gets paid off, the more quickly it amortizes any discount in the original purchase price.

To track the return profile of a BB Note, various take-out scenarios are considered (0 months post-RP all the way through 72 months post-RP, which would represent the full amortization of the deal). While the market trades around Discount Margins that assume the BB Note goes its full duration, this rarely occurs, and deals are often reset, refinanced, or called well ahead of this terminal date. When evaluating a potential BB Note investment, it's important to have a view on how long the deal will remain outstanding, as this can significantly change the expected return profile. This is especially true for CLO BBs purchased at steep discounts to par.

The default rate required to break the BB Note is tracked, assuming it goes through a full amortization (this is the most draconian scenario as leveraged loans continue to default every year for a longer period of time). The BB Note "breaking" is defined as incurring any loss of principal; in this analysis, a high IRR in a "broken" BB is still possible. This statistic is calculated assuming both a 70% recovery rate and a 50% recovery rate on the leverage loans.

Below are some examples of BBs with various profiles that traded around the same time. Key metrics are broken out to show how they influence the levels at which the bonds trade.

Deal	Description	Price	MVOC	Par Sub	Years since R/P End	DM	IRR - 36 Months Post RP Call	IRR - 72 Months Post RP Call	Def rate to break with 70% recov
#1	Long-Dated BSL / High MVOC	93.09%	103.79%	8.60%	-3.51	813	12.09%	11.70%	7.00%
#2	Short-Dated BSL / High MVOC	90.83%	103.51%	7.00%	1.70	926	19.57%	13.03%	13.00%
#3	Short-Dated BSL / Low MVOC	82.81%	100.44%	6.29%	0.46	1,077	19.15%	14.47%	5.00%
#4	Short-Dated Middle Market	93.25%	N/A	14.18%	-0.26	1,006	14.90%	14.30%	25.00%
#5	Long-Dated Middle Market	92.25%	N/A	12.26%	-3.20	1,039	15.04%	14.61%	14.00%

- Deals #1 and #2 are both high-MVOC BSL BBs, indicating that the underlying portfolios are performing well, but #1 still has a long time to go before its reinvestment period ends. Deal #2 is already 1.7 years past its reinvestment period. Deal #2 has a par sub of 7% (vs. 8% when the deal started), showing that during the life of the CLO there has been some moderate par burn.
  - Despite the lower par sub, Deal #2 survives significantly higher default levels than Deal #1—this is because the length of the deal is considerably shorter, and the default rates are being sustained over a shorter period for Deal #2.
  - Deal #1 traded at a tighter DM than Deal #2—the market for high-quality, long-dated BBs is generally better bid than other profiles, but this difference could also come down to manager preference or other factors.

o   Note that the difference between the IRR to a call 36 months post-RP for these deals is significant. Because these bonds are bought at discounts, the shorter-dated BB (Deal #2) will reach the call date more quickly and realize the gain when the BB repays at par, enhancing the IRR in that scenario.

- Deals #2 and #3 are both short-dated BSL BBs but Deal #3 has a significantly lower MVOC and Par Sub when compared to Deal #2. This results in lower survival metrics, as there is less of an equity buffer to absorb loan losses. Deal #3 traded at a significantly wider DM than Deal #2, reflecting the increased risk of principal loss.

- Deals #4 and #5 are Middle Market BBs, with Deal #4 being short-dated and Deal #5 being long-dated. As noted above, the length of the CLO significantly impacts the survival metrics, and the DMs at which they traded reflect this.

Before buying a CLO BB Note, the indenture needs to be checked for language regarding reinvestment post reinvestment period end. The more restrictive the language, the faster the deal will be expected to be called. Since CLO BB Notes are usually bought at a discount, restrictive language favors the BB Note, while more permissive language favors the CLO Equity.

13.10 B Notes

A CLO issues a B Note about 8% of the time. The reason is it's an expensive part of the CLO's debt financing. Usually, its spread would be 2.0% higher than the BB Note, and sold at a discount to par value. From the equity investor's perspective, the typical preference is not to issue the B Note, and instead have a greater percentage of the CLO financed with equity.

However, there are times when the B Note would make sense to issue:

- The B Note is done at attractive levels, so its issuance is accretive to equity returns.
- The B Note would reduce the cash contribution of an equity investor who might be short of funds.
- The CLO equity investor may decide to have the B Note structured into the CLO but retain the entire tranche. That would allow the investor to sell the B Note in the future, if desired.

Regarding credit quality, the B Note is often considered a preferred equity investment, given the quantity of CLO Notes that are senior to it. But the B Note only gets its quarterly contractual interest, while the CLO equity investors may receive cash-on-cash payments in the high teens.

Common Mistakes in CLO Investing

14.1 Lessons Learned

During my career, I've seen lots of mistakes in CLO investing. Here are some rules I think are useful:

- CLO Equity investing, in particular, is not a great investment for investors that do not already have deep relationships in the market.

  Imagine a CLO arranger has a $50 million equity tranche to sell in a new CLO. Who gets the first look? Given the investment size, the arranger generally cannot show the opportunity to multiple potential investors simultaneously. That's because each investor may want a majority of the equity, and if they all want the deal, several will be disappointed. So, the arranger starts with one account, and if that account declines, he moves on to the second. The pecking order is established by who does the most business with the arranger, among other factors. As a result, people new to the CLO asset class will find themselves at the bottom of the pecking order and will only see CLO opportunities that multiple others have passed on.

  Similarly, an investor must see other relevant market trades before making an investment. If you see a one-off trade from a broker-dealer, it may end up being a fine investment, but you need to make sure you pay a fair price that is in line with recent market transactions.

- An investor in CLO Equity should approach the market with the broadest possible mandate.

Many investors who want exposure to CLOs invest with one CLO manager in a GP/LP fund format that will invest in the next several CLO Equity tranches managed by that manager. This is an easy but inefficient way to invest. The investible universe of CLO Equity tranches is over 1,600 deals. Primary CLOs, secondary CLOs, CLO warehouses, and Middle Market CLOs are all options. An investor in a GP/LP manager fund will target the smallest fraction of the investible market, and there will be a high overlap of the leveraged loans in each CLO. Slowly waiting for the GP/LP fund to call capital may also be undesirable.

- A CLO manager may not make the best CLO Equity investor.

Many CLO Equity investors are also CLO managers, and they effectively market their CLO management skill as being useful in picking the best CLO Equity investments. However, this can quickly result in some conflicts of interest. Is the CLO Equity investor really looking at the whole market for the best CLO equity opportunities, or is he simply helping the home team by investing in his firm's CLOs? Let's say the CLO manager has syndicated almost all the CLO Notes for a new deal, but a few unsold parts of the capital structure remain. Perhaps those unwanted securities will end up in the CLO Equity Fund?

- CLO BB Notes are robust, even when the MVOC is less than 100%.

When the leveraged loan market sells off, potential returns in BB Notes can be equity-like, with a fraction of the risk. On its face, investing in a CLO BB Note seems very risky when, if the CLO was hypothetically liquidated, the proceeds would not fully cover the BB Note. But few CLO BBs have defaulted, and there are two ways that the MVOC likely ends up above 100%, which is a requirement to get a full repayment on the CLO BB Note. First, many of the CLO's leveraged loans will repay at par, thus increasing the market value coverage over time, as the leveraged loans' fair value is typically below par. Second, if the CLO's leveraged loans materially underperform, the diversion of cash flow that would have otherwise gone to the equity will also benefit the market value coverage. Do not underestimate the value of this CLO structural protection for the BB Note.

- Allocation to Middle Market CLO Equity and BB Notes can potentially reduce overall portfolio risk.

Middle market CLOs offer exposure to a unique set of levered loans that aren't represented in broadly syndicated CLOs. Projected equity returns are comparable to CLOs backed by broadly syndicated loans, but middle market equity tends to retain its value better in down markets. That's because changes in the fair value of middle market CLO Equity are primarily driven by the actual performance of the underlying middle market loans. In contrast, technical factors influence the broadly syndicated leveraged loan market.

Additionally, middle market BB Notes offer a 1–2% return premium above broadly syndicated BB Notes, while the middle market BBs benefit from ~ 4% of additional equity in the CLO.

Market Participant Perspectives

15.1 Drew Sweeney, TCW, Broadly Syndicated Loan Manager

Mr. Sweeney is a Managing Director in the Fixed Income Group, where he serves as a portfolio manager and trader for the TCW CLOs and the MetWest Floating Rate Income Fund. Mr. Sweeney was previously a portfolio manager at Bradford & Marzec, LLC and Macquarie Group (FKA Four Corners Capital Management) for separately managed accounts, closed-end funds, and CLO accounts. Prior to Four Corners, he worked as a research analyst evaluating leveraged loan and bond investments for Columbia Management (Ameriprise Financial, Inc.) and ING Capital Advisors. Mr. Sweeney has also worked in investment banking at Wells Fargo Securities (FKA First Union), where he focused on underwriting, structuring, and syndicating leveraged loan transactions within the sponsor origination and consumer product groups. He holds a BS from Rutgers University and an MBA from the University of North Carolina Kenan-Flagler Business School.

When did TCW start managing CLOs?

TCW has managed CLOs for over a decade; however, the most recent team began managing CLOs at TCW in 2013.

How many CLOs / Loans do you manage?

As of December 2022, TCW managed eight CLOs and approximately $6 billion in total loans.

Why do you think CLOs are attractive?

I believe investors need to allocate to a variety of investments, and CLO equity can provide an uncorrelated equity-like return. It can be part of every asset allocation when an investor introduces risk to a portfolio. Despite improved liquidity within the leveraged loan market, CLOs will continue to have a vintage bias, meaning some time periods in CLO investments will perform better than other periods. Consequently, the optimal way to benefit from the CLO market is programmatic investing over a long period of time. This is not different than the way employees add a monthly contribution to a 401k account.

Why do you think investors choose TCW?

TCW provides a large, well-capitalized diversified manager that can dedicate resources to the CLO platform even when CLO inflows are limited. More specifically, TCW offers best-in-class asset management and research to enhance performance. Finally, TCW has a defined and differentiated process that allows investors to benefit from an investment style that does not resemble other managers:

- The CLO credit team is integrated into the broader credit platform.

- It's a consensus-driven, team-based process that seeks to question investment assumptions at every level of the firm.
- We have built and maintained a research database, which includes a large percentage of the investable leveraged loan universe. This is unique and helps inform our investment process.
- We overlap the investment process with a consistent fund optimization process that drives consistent par build.

15.2 Kelli Marti, Churchill Asset Management, Middle Market CLO Manager

Kelli Marti is a Senior Managing Director at Churchill and serves as Head of CLO Management, and is a member of Churchill's Operating Committee. Kelli is responsible for the management and growth of Churchill's Middle Market CLO platform, including day-to-day vehicle oversight, assisting in sourcing assets and trading strategy development, as well as participating in fundraising initiatives. Before joining Churchill, Kelli spent eighteen years at Crestline Denali Capital, a CLO asset manager. Most recently, she served as Crestline Denali's Managing Director and Chief Credit Officer, where she was responsible for overseeing the firm's entire credit function, including new business underwriting and portfolio management. She also served on the firm's Investment Committee. Prior to joining Crestline Denali, Kelli was a Vice President at Heller Financial, where she was responsible for underwriting and managing middle market loans. Before joining Heller, she was an Assistant Vice President at First Source Financial, where she underwrote direct middle market transactions on behalf of the firm's CLO portfolio. She began her career as an auditor at KPMG in Chicago.

Kelli graduated magna cum laude with a BS in Accounting from the University of Notre Dame, and received her MBA with high honors from the Kellogg School of Management at Northwestern University. She previously earned her CPA certification.

When did Churchill start managing middle market CLOs?

Churchill Asset Management is a long-time CLO manager, having closed its first middle market CLO, Churchill Financial Cayman, in 2007, at $1.25 billion, under Churchill's predecessor firm, Churchill Financial. At its launch, Churchill Financial Cayman Ltd. was established to leverage exposure to middle market loans in a long-term vehicle with locked-up attractive financing. The Churchill Financial team successfully managed Churchill Cayman Financial Ltd. through the credit crisis of 2008 through 2010, ultimately achieving an IRR above 17%. Since launching Churchill Asset Management LLC as an affiliate of TIAA/Nuveen in 2015, Churchill has continued to manage CLOs and other senior lending initiatives.

Currently, Churchill issues both arbitrage CLOs (Notes from AAA-BB issued) and financing CLOs for its levered funds or business development companies (Notes AAA-A issued). Regardless of the CLO structure, we look to have well-structured CLO warehouses with adequate tenor in place. This allows us to be patient in times of slower origination and/or volatility in the capital markets that would make issuances challenging. Importantly, TIAA holds the majority equity position in all the arbitrage CLOs issued by Churchill.

How many CLOs do you manage?

Churchill currently manages three closed-arbitrage middle market CLOs as well as two closed-financing CLO transactions, Churchill NCDLC CLO-I, LLC and Churchill MMSLF CLO-I, LP.

For our upcoming CLO issuances, we continue to ramp and aggregate assets for various arbitrage and financing CLOs.

Why do you think CLOs are attractive?

I believe CLOs are attractive for a number of reasons, particularly (i) the ability to attract a wide range of investors, (ii) the structural protections provided to investors, and (iii) the attractive returns and low default rates demonstrated over the past 25+ years. CLOs attract a wide range of investors, including but not limited to regional and foreign banks, insurance companies, pension funds and endowments, hedge funds, and money managers due to the multiple tranches of rated debt as well as equity in the capital stack. For investors desiring lower risk, higher par subordination, and that need to meet regulatory requirements, the AAA and AA Senior Notes of a CLO would be attractive. The mezzanine debt tranches (A/BBB/BB) would be attractive for investors desiring higher return in exchange for higher risk, but ascribe value to having a rated debt instrument. Finally, those investors seeking the highest return and potential upside but willing to undertake the highest risk would find CLO equity a compelling investment. CLOs generally have a low correlation to other fixed income categories, which helps to increase the diversification of investors' portfolios.

CLOs are structured with built-in risk protections for their investors, including collateral concentration limits, borrower diversification requirements, collateral quality tests and coverage tests. These tests, including a limitation on assets with a rating of CCC/Caa or below, as well as O/C tests, are in place to ensure that the manager is accumulating and managing a diverse portfolio of well-performing loan investments. To the extent the underlying portfolio experiences weakness over a certain threshold, the indenture requires a redirection of cash flow to repay the highest-rated debt tranches first. The CLO manager is required to demonstrate compliance with its coverage tests and collateral quality covenants monthly and must report these compliance metrics to its investors.

While CLOs are not without complexities, investors are rewarded for taking the time to understand these complexities and accepting lower liquidity in their investments in exchange for higher returns. CLO debt tranches are priced at a premium compared to similarly rated corporate bonds, and equity returns of CLOs are typically in the mid to high-teens area, providing very attractive risk-adjusted returns. Further, default rates in CLO Notes have been negligible.

Why do you think investors choose Churchill?

With a history dating back to 2006 and $46 billion in committed capital under management, Churchill is one of the most established players in middle market institutional lending. Some of our key competitive advantages include:

- Premier sponsorship. Churchill benefits from the scale and resources of our parent company, Nuveen, which manages over $1.1 trillion of assets, including $85 billion in private capital (as of September 30, 2022).
- Firm alignment. Churchill's ultimate parent company, TIAA, invests side-by-side with our third-party investors, on average committing to 30% of each transaction underwritten by Churchill.
- Experienced and deep management. Our senior management team averages nearly 30 years of middle market lending experience.
- Cycle-tested track record. Over its 17+ years of investing, Churchill has demonstrated a strong track record with very

low loss ratios. Churchill has shown its ability to effectively invest across market cycles, having funded $27.4 billion of senior loans in 787 transactions since 2006 (as of 30 Sep 2022).

- Unique relationship-driven origination model. Churchill's Private Equity and Junior Capital team has invested $12 billion as a limited partner in over 260 private equity funds, primarily middle market focused, driving robust deal flow. Importantly, Churchill is viewed by the GP community as a strategic partner due to its consistent private equity investing.

- Conservative approach. Churchill is highly selective, issuing senior secured loans with structural protections, including financial covenants and modest leverage to middle market borrowers with superior operating management and top-tier private equity sponsorship. Further, Churchill protects against the downside through a highly diversified portfolio, with average hold sizes per investment of less than 1% per vehicle.

As a top lead agent in the middle market, our private equity relationships and competitive edge continue to strengthen, particularly as Churchill is an incumbent agent on an increasing number of transactions (currently ~ 70%). The Firm's increased leadership position highlights Churchill's strong position in the middle market as a trusted partner for private equity firms. These competitive advantages allow Churchill to see the widest possible range of transactions in the market while remaining highly disciplined, with a loan approval rate of only ~7%. Churchill's strong track record reflects its conservative approach to its underwriting and portfolio management.

Process for sourcing middle market loans

As mentioned, Churchill sources middle market investment opportunities primarily through the firm's network of relationships with private equity firms. Churchill's origination team has offices across the US, including New York, Chicago, and Los Angeles, to enhance their ability to maintain frequent sponsor connectivity. Churchill believes that the strength and breadth of the investment team's relationships, enhanced by the firm's role as a significant LP investor in middle market private equity funds, enable the firm to maximize deal flow, support a highly selective investment process, and establish favorable portfolio diversification.

Churchill's investment philosophy rests on the belief that superior risk-adjusted returns are available to direct lenders who can successfully access top tier middle market private equity-sponsored borrowers with stable and consistent cash flows. Churchill believes a conservative approach to direct lending is prudent regarding covenants, borrower leverage, and sponsorship. Churchill's senior lending investment vehicles, including the CLOs, are focused on investing in senior secured loans to private equity-owned US-based middle market companies. These companies typically require capital for growth, acquisitions, recapitalizations, refinancings, or leveraged buyouts.

15.3 Chris Gilbert, Natixis, CLO Arranger

Chris Gilbert is a Managing Director at Natixis and Head of US CLO Banking. Chris is responsible for overseeing Natixis' business of using structured credit technologies to finance portfolios of corporate loans, both in capital markets transactions and in private bilateral and club facilities. Natixis is the US leader in arranging middle market CLOs and a strong participant in the broadly syndicated CLO market as well. Chris joined Natixis in 2005 and has been primarily focused on CLOs and related private facilities.

Prior to joining Natixis, Chris served as both an investment banker focusing on the technology industry and a corporate credit analyst at Goldman Sachs. Before that, Chris was employed by Peterson Consulting, primarily focused on financial and accounting work for the Resolution Trust Corporation.

Chris earned an MBA from the Darden School of Business at the University of Virginia and a B.B.A. from the College of William & Mary. He also holds a designation as a Chartered Financial Analyst.

Why did you gravitate towards CLOs?

Initially, my entry into the CLO market was opportunistic. A former colleague from my credit and corporate finance days at Goldman Sachs had moved to Natixis and recommended me to the successful team here. As I reviewed the opportunity, I was drawn to the analytic foundation of structured credit and how it meshed with my corporate credit and corporate finance background. The connection to both underlying corporate loan assets and the strategic planning for middle market lending platforms that use CLOs to finance their corporate lending business was a strong fit for my experience and interests. Fortunately, the industry has weathered the volatility of past crises quite well, and Natixis has demonstrated a sustained dedication to the business, which permitted me to continue to deepen my involvement in the CLO market.

Ultimately, the many fantastic people I have met along the way have made my career in CLOs so rewarding. I have been fortunate in developing strong connections with many of the outstanding people in the CLO market, including colleagues throughout Natixis, CLO managers, investors, and the many other constituents that create the vibrant community that drives our industry.

How do you decide which managers to work with?

There are many considerations in determining which managers we want to target, such as the profile of the manager, the tone in the market, and whether the transaction is for a CLO of broadly syndicated loans or a CLO of middle market/directly originated loans.

A key first criterion is selecting a manager that has a visible path to transaction execution. Managers with a strong investor following in both equity and debt are good candidates as it gives clarity of execution. That following is generally a result of strong historic performance as well as being repeat issuers to give an element of liquidity to secondary trading in their deals. There can be tension between a manager's perceived risk tolerance for debt investors that may prefer a more conservative style and a perception from equity investors on a willingness to take appropriate risks to help to generate a strong return for equity investors; however, the most sought-after managers have demonstrated an ability to deliver strong returns across markets while maintaining a relatively conservative portfolio. In addition, manager tiering can arise in debt pricing due to concerns about secondary liquidity (related to the frequency of CLO issuance or broader investor acceptance of the name), the depth of a manager's credit resources, or the work required to onboard a new manager and their related transaction documents. If a perception of manager tiering impacts debt pricing, the direct impact on returns will reduce the visibility of execution unless a manager can bring his or her own equity investors. If equity or anchor AAA investors express interest in working with a specific manager, we will often be able to expedite a trade and work with the parties to match this reverse inquiry.

In addition, Natixis strives to connect with managers that can be repeat clients. With over 140 active BSL CLO Managers and around 30 active middle market managers, we do not feel that we can effectively engage with the full set of managers with the level of partnership that we target. We have found that repeat transactions with a manager can lead to significant efficiencies in execution. Our sales force learns to intelligently articulate and distinguish managers' styles and track records as well as to best match investor preferences to manager strategies. Our banking team will have advance notice of portfolio construction nuances and how best to match structures and transaction terms. Our syndicate desk will develop an intuitive sense of how the transaction will likely progress and where to focus marketing to achieve the best result in execution. In addition, occasional tax, operational or other nuances can complicate execution for certain managers. Being able to address these early in the transaction's life and to rely on past solutions can improve the execution timeline and experience.

We also seek to offer a diverse range of managers to investors that may seek different profiles in their investments. Some investors seek managers with the highest spread at a given rating. Others may seek tighter portfolio construction rules, while others may prefer higher par subordination, often accompanying structures with more flexibility on portfolio construction.

When considering managers for middle market/direct lending CLOs, we also focus on lenders with a reliable, consistent source of origination to ensure that the portfolio ramp can meet expectations from both a timing and quality perspective. In these CLOs, strong work-out capabilities are often required because direct lenders typically do not have the option to trade out of loans when the manager's view on credit changes. A long history of credit experience will be important to demonstrate a direct lender's access to credits, stability of underwriting standards, and portfolio monitoring and work-out capabilities across cycles.

Finally, other strategic relationships between the bank and a manager's broader platform and any potential reputational risks will also be considered when pursuing a mandate with a manager.

How do you differentiate yourself as a CLO underwriter?

At Natixis, we work hard to differentiate ourselves as a CLO underwriter primarily through excellent execution and efficient financing terms.

Excellence of execution is driven by a deep knowledge of the markets and current investor interest across the addressable market. Constant dialog with a wide range of investors by the sales force, the syndication team, and the CLO team generally permits us to match the unique needs of investors with opportunities that specific managers can offer. For example, if there are investors with specific needs for shorter-term exposures, we can match with a portfolio that may have a unique need for shorter-term financing such as a fixed-life fund nearing the end of its investment period. Also, investors with specific demands for equity (e.g., optimizing returns by focusing on costs, sourcing more unique direct lending opportunities with unique tax structures, or specific needs with respect to ramping portfolios in particular ways) can lead to opportunities to connect with different managers.

Excellence of execution is also driven by deep structuring and operational capabilities. Natixis maintains a large structuring team with deep experience focused on CLOs that can provide expert advice that can be tailored to several unique situations. Our team has deep knowledge of rating criteria for both BSL and Middle Market CLOs, experience with tax issues that may arise (particularly for Middle Market CLOs[1]), and work-out flexibility required for syndicated and directly originated loans. In addition, we focus on ensuring that the portfolio construction flexibility provided by a transaction accurately matches the strategic goals of the manager and their portfolio acquisition (trading or direct lending) and portfolio management (active, passive, trading, activist) strategies.

Excellence of execution also involves retaining strong credibility with investors across deals and cycles to ensure that investors prioritize focus on deals brought to the market by Natixis in times of heavy new issue activity. Maintaining a transparent marketing and allocation process and acting as a credible counterparty with both managers and investors are crucial to obtaining and

---

[1] Natixis does not provide tax, legal, or accounting advice. Consult your advisors. Given our experience in the market, we are happy to suggest a long list of competent law firms, accounting firms, valuation firms, or rating agencies.

maintaining the focus of investors to prioritize deals brought to the market. In addition, Natixis' strong presence in both BSL and Middle Market CLOs[2] allows us to show investors a differentiated offering that meets a wide range of investor demands.

In addition to ensuring excellence of execution, Natixis focuses on providing well-structured financing to managers and equity investors throughout the transaction's life. This involves having one or more flexible warehouse structures that reflect the nature of the portfolio being assembled, the needs of the equity/first loss investor(s), and motivation being paired with the warehouse lenders. Warehouses need sufficient flexibility to match the manager's portfolio strategy, which can vary significantly among various managers and their platforms. In addition, warehouse structures must provide sufficient flexibility to be relevant across changes in the market environment to give all parties confidence that the financing will permit the manager the time it takes to ramp a portfolio that will permit a successful securitization. While the initial warehouse structure is crucial to giving managers and investors comfort on market risk, Natixis' attitude towards partnership and flexibility during unforeseen events has been vital in differentiating ourselves as an arranger. At Natixis, the CLO business has a prominent place in our practice. Historically, our structured credit business has been larger than our leveraged finance business. As a result, we have not been a group that supports leveraged finance to provide captive buyers of new syndicated loans into CLOs or warehouses. Further, our CLO business is larger than our Asset Backed Securities business in the US, helping to keep the sales force focused on CLO distribution as a primary product. As a

---

[2] Natixis has consistently been in the top 10 arrangers of US CLOs consistently over the past 4 years and the top 1 or 2 arrangers of Middle Market CLOs over the past 5+ years as tracked by CreditFlux.

result, the business has the strong focus of senior management and a highly skilled risk team that is experienced in finding solutions that work for both Natixis and our clients in times of stress in the market. For example, Natixis was extending and growing warehouse facilities in March through May 2020 during the peak of the COVID-19 crisis in the market. At that time, we heard that other arrangers were focused on actively reducing exposures to warehouses. In addition, management selectively deploys the balance sheet to capital market transactions via our active CLO trading desk and our hold-to-collect banking book. Natixis has been an arranger of CLOs since 2003 and has never liquidated or accelerated any warehouse or related financing facility. The business entered the Great Financial Crisis with a significant book of positions and did not accelerate any of those (or suffer any losses on any of them.) That partnership and enduring commitment are primary factors that have contributed to our ability to maintain our top two position on the middle market CLO league tables for the past decade.

What is the most challenging part of bringing a CLO to life?

The most challenging part of arranging a CLO will vary dramatically in different market conditions and the motivations of the key players in the CLO (Collateral Manager, Equity Investor, AAA anchor, etc.)

Often, we see a different set of significant challenges between broadly syndicated CLOs and middle market CLOs. These can stem from the primary motivations of the CLO (arbitrage trade versus a financing trade), portfolio flexibility required by a manager's strategy or return, and leverage requirements of the transaction.

At some points in the market, the arbitrage expressed as the return expected to be received by equity in a transaction will be below (and potentially well below) where equity investors would target for the level of risk expected (as discussed elsewhere in this book.) AAA Note capacity may be constrained at other points in the market as large anchor investors may have reduced capacity when compared to the supply of transactions seeking market execution. In addition, the price and terms of loans warehoused in a benign environment may be challenging to make sense to finance in volatile markets when debt spreads rapidly widen. When the arbitrage is in a weak position, it can be challenging to place equity in a new issue broadly syndicated CLO or have warehouse first loss investors seek to term out their positions.

At any given point in the market, there is often a tranche that is the most difficult to place. While the arbitrage for BSL CLOs may be difficult from time to time, the supply-and-demand mechanics of the CLO market and leveraged loan market (of which CLOs are the largest investor) tend to bring the arbitrage back to levels that permit new execution over time.

Alternatively, middle market CLOs are less dependent on a point in time arbitrage. Middle market/direct lenders often win mandates to deliver a levered return based on an originated portfolio of private corporate loans delivered by the manager's proprietary origination and management platform. In these cases, the direct lender manager will assemble a portfolio of loans that may be suitable for a CLO over a period of multiple years, supported by a warehouse provided by an arranger or perhaps ramped without leverage on the investor's balance sheet. Once the portfolio is assembled, the direct lender will often be faced with the option to either finance this portfolio via the bank lending market or the CLO market. In this case, the decision is often less of evaluating a point in time arbitrage as it's evaluating the cost-effectiveness and capacity of the bank market and comparing it to the CLO market. The manager will typically have discretion as to which of these to choose based on the expected cost and reliability of the financing options.

In addition to market capacity for all tranches, gaining investor focus can be a significant challenge during frenetic periods in the market when significant supply is competing for the attention of investors. Beyond the key market and investor dynamics, specific technical factors can be a challenge for execution, including periods in the market in which one or more rating agencies may lack the capacity to process transactions at the rate required by the market. In addition, regulatory focus on specific structures may disrupt timing or execution plans (e.g., NAIC scrutiny on combo notes or risk retention rules in various jurisdictions.)

15.4 Brad Larson, Credit Suisse, CLO Arranger

Authors Note: As of June 2023, Brad became head of CLO arranging at CIBC.

I began my undergraduate education at the University of California at Berkeley. I received a BA in Legal Studies while competing for Cal's Division I soccer team. After graduation, my interest in finance grew, and I earned a Master of Science in Management ("MSM") at the Krannert Graduate School of Management at Purdue University.

My investment banking career began at Prudential Securities in New York. In this role at Prudential, I gained my first experience with securitization financing. My work in finance and securitized products led to roles at aircraft lessor Pegasus Aviation and financial guarantor and asset manager ACA. After several years involved in CLOs on the buy-side, my sell-side CLO career was launched at Credit Suisse in 2010. At Credit Suisse, I helped start and develop the bank's post-Global Financial Crisis return to the CLO arranging market.

I am currently Global Head of the CLO New Issue Group at Credit Suisse. Over the last 12 years, I have overseen teams in New York and London that have completed more than 350 US and European CLO transactions across more than 75 managers.

Why did you gravitate towards CLOs?

Early in my finance career, I found the ingenuity and practical application of securitization financing compelling. At a time when the securitization market occupied a more obscure corner of finance, I had a strong hunch that I wanted to be involved. Securitization represented a source of efficient financing for an issuing company while often simultaneously offering a better relative value investment for investors. Therefore, securitization made sense from both supply and demand perspectives, and I believed there would be lasting demand. However, what really drew me to CLOs was how well the CLO structure performed through the financial crisis.

CLOs are long-term structures not subject to short-term redemptions or outflow pressures that can be seen in retail funds or liquidating separately managed accounts. Structurally, in times of stress, CLOs have tests and rules to shift cash flows away from the riskiest tranche to those less risky to protect against defaults. This self-healing mechanism keeps the deal in place as a source of stable funding and potential market liquidity. Further, because loans provide operating capital to companies and companies create jobs, loans can be seen as an important part of our economy and labor market. I believed if loans had sustainable relevance, so would CLOs.

How do you decide which managers to work with?

To some extent, I rely on gut instinct when determining which managers to work with. Some aspects are obvious (e.g., manager size, history, and other institutional touchpoints), but I also base my decisions on feel and chemistry. Do I know the individuals well? Is the manager a good personality fit for me and the team? Does the manager's message match the metrics (i.e., have they done all they say they have done)? Do I believe there is potential for a long-term partnership? How positive has the manager interaction experience been with my colleagues and/or clients and service providers? Is the manager introspective? CLOs have been around for a long time, and the community is small. Therefore, while this initial screen rarely would lead to an outright "pass," I do want to have a personal view of the potential dynamics, challenges, and opportunities prior to taking on a mandate. However, there are performance, style, and market-specific considerations as well.

I want to clearly understand the manager's management style and performance history. What is the manager's credit process and team size? What is the manager's tranche downgrade history? How are historical WARF scores? Is the manager high spread/low spread? High diversity/low diversity? Frequent trader/infrequent trader? More defensive/more offensive? Are there any manager legacy issues in the market that are cause for concern? What are the manager's historical equity returns (cash on cash, total return, final IRR)? Is the manager perceived as more equity-friendly or debt-friendly? How do the manager's bonds trade? What is the general liquidity like? Will the manager take all/any equity, typically the hardest tranche to sell? What is the manager's historical AAA (often the next hardest tranche to sell) buyer base?

While there are few outright disqualifying responses to any of the questions above, the answers will influence mandate timing, pipeline positioning, and the deal type best pursued. The origination process is thorough and designed to maximize the likelihood of success and ensure the client relationship remains intact by the end of the deal.

How do you differentiate yourself as a CLO Arranger?

An arranger's ability to structure and document a deal is a baseline expectation. While some arrangers are better than others, the differentiation among arrangers in terms of structuring a deal is typically insignificant. However, there are other distinguishing aspects important to note:

- attractive warehouse terms (usually longer-term maturities, higher advance rates and/or lower financing rates)
- ability to underwrite certain tranches (e.g., AAA or equity) in a deal
- loan origination or trading capabilities
- CLO sales and syndication capabilities
- CLO equity placement capabilities

At Credit Suisse, I generally do not compete on warehouse terms, and our business has never really had much appetite for AAA or equity underwrites. On occasion, we have sponsored portions of minority equity, but never as a formal business strategy or competitive advantage. Where we do try to distinguish ourselves, though, is in CLO sales and syndication and CLO equity placement with third parties. I believe our manager and client preparation, work rate, and unique relationships are the difference-maker in these areas.

What is the most challenging part of bringing a CLO to life?

Many in the industry would argue that selling the equity is the most challenging part of bringing a CLO to life. Certainly, selling equity is, at times, the most challenging aspect of the process, and selling AAAs can also be quite difficult. However, I believe the real challenge is coordinating multiple parties with differing motivations and incentives to secure pricing commitments. Further, given that planning, organization, and commitments often need execution within a tight timeframe (e.g., usually about two weeks), in an ever-changing market, bringing a CLO to life is a minor miracle in the best of environments.

A CLO mandate always starts with a manager, an engagement letter, and warehouse agreement. Sometimes 100% of the equity is "committed" upfront; sometimes it's 51%; and sometimes less. Rarely is it zero. The primary loan market is typically the main source for loans for the warehouse. This newly underwritten collateral comes at a current market spread and usually at a discount to par. However, sometimes secondary loans are preferred for the deal, depending on secondary market loan pricing,

Subject to the warehouse build; the CLO equity placement strategy (has it been committed upfront, or is an additional equity raise required?); the CLO liability market conditions; and the strategy for AAA placement (sometimes an "anchor" AAA is the plan and sometimes a syndicated approach is the plan), the arranger, manager, and equity may decide to proceed. However, even after they decide to proceed, loans usually must be purchased by the manager at or better than modeled in the "go/no-go" decision. Further, CLO liabilities need to be sold by the arranger at or better than modelled (absent any positive benefit achieved on loan purchases by the manager). And realize that negotiating the terms of the CLO liability sale typically takes two to four weeks. All the while loan prices and liability levels can change, which can bring the parties back to the "go/no-go" decision again.

Given all the variables and constantly moving parts, the expression "herding cats" often comes to mind and, hence, my view on coordination being the biggest challenge.

How does CLO secondary trading tie into your business?

CLO secondary trading ties into the primary business in several ways, and though the groups function separately, I view them as importantly linked. Clearly, without primary there is no secondary. However, given CLOs do not trade on an exchange, secondary trading is fundamental to a healthy primary market in that it offers a source of liquidity to original-issuance investors. In other words, a secondary capability provides investors with the comfort that if they need to sell prior to maturity they should have an exit option.

Secondary trading is also important to my primary business from a market intelligence perspective. Many CLO investors today can buy both primary and secondary and will buy based on the best relative value. Therefore, having a desk in touch with the movements of the market allows us to advise our issuer clients appropriately on timing and pricing. To the extent secondary pricing levels are trending tight to primary, this may represent an opportunity to tighten pricing and go to market as demand may be higher for primary relative to secondary. Obviously, the opposite can also be true. However, the better informed we are on the market, the better we can advise our managers on an issuance strategy.

Finally, many clients require monthly or quarterly valuations on their CLO positions purchased. The secondary desk is the group that provides our clients with their valuations. This is an important function for many accounts, using those valuations to report on their fund performance.

Conclusion

I hope this has given a helpful description of asset classes I believe have attractive risk-adjusted return characteristics. As the CLO market continues to grow, investment professionals who work outside of CLOs must have a basic understanding of this market. If, after reading this, you don't find CLO equity or CLO BB-rated notes to be a compelling investment, you may be interested in buying one of the other CLO Notes or even leveraged loans outside of the CLO structure. In CLOs, there is usually a trade for everyone.

Glossary

AAA Note – a type of debt security issued by a CLO with the highest possible credit rating assigned by a credit rating agency, typically Moody's or S&P; makes up the largest dollar amount, lowest risk, and lowest return profile of a CLO's debt securities

Amortization – scheduled mandatory repayments of a borrower's debt, usually 1% annually for leveraged loans with a lump sum payment due at maturity

Arbitrage CLO – A CLO whose objective is to make a favorable return for the CLO equity owners

Balance Sheet CLO – A CLO used to finance leveraged loans owned in a loan fund, or Business Development Company

Bid-Ask Spread – the difference between the highest price a buyer is willing to pay (bid) for a financial instrument and the lowest price a seller is willing to accept (ask) for the same instrument at a given point in time

Bids Wanted In Competition (BWICs) – semi-public secondary auctions for a package of securities submitted by an institutional investor to securities dealers to request bids from their clients

Broadly Syndicated Loans – large corporate loans underwritten by investment banks and syndicated, or sold, in smaller pieces to a large group (usually multiple dozen) of third-party financial institutions such as loan mutual funds, hedge funds, and CLOs

Central Clearing House – an entity that helps facilitate securities trades between counterparties in financial transactions

CLO Arranger – the investment bank that underwrites, structures, and arranges the issuance of a CLO

CLO Equity – the riskiest tranche of a CLO but also the portion with the highest return potential; investors typically include the CLO's manager and/or other institutional investors, and these groups maintain certain rights that investors in the debt tranches do not have, such as the right to call a CLO or to refinance its debt; used to finance around 10% of a CLO's loan purchases

CLO Indenture – the legal document that outlines the terms and conditions of a CLO and governs the relationship between the CLO issuer and the trustee who represents the interests of the investors in the CLO

CLO Manager – the organization responsible for managing the assets of a CLO, including selecting the underlying loans

CLO Notes – the different debt tranches that are issued as part of a CLO and vary based on credit quality and return profile; used to finance around 90% of a typical CLO

CLO Trustee – a third-party entity responsible for administering a CLO on behalf of the investors in the CLO; acts as an intermediary between the CLO manager and the investors, ensuring that the terms of the CLO are adhered to and that the interests of the investors are protected

CLO Warehouse – a short-term financing vehicle provided by an investment bank to CLO managers to accumulate a pool of leveraged loans that will eventually be securitized into a CLO

Collateral – the assets that a borrower pledges to a lender as security

Collateralized Debt Obligations (CDO) – a type of structured financial product that pools together a large number of individual debt securities, such as bonds or loans, and creates different tranches or layers of securities that have varying levels of risk and return

Compliance Certificate – a document that a borrower submits to a lender to confirm that the borrower complies with the terms and conditions of a loan agreement

Constant Default Rate (CDR) – a CLO modeling assumption representing the percentage of loans expected to default annually over the life of a CLO

Cover Bid – second highest bid, which is often published to the market in a BWIC auction

Covenants – conditions or restrictions on the activities of a borrower included in a loan or bond agreement issuance designed to protect the interests of the lender or bondholder

Covenant-Lite – refers to a type of loan or bond that contains fewer or less stringent financial covenants than traditional loan or bond agreements

Credit Agreement – the legal document of terms and conditions that govern the relationship between a lender and borrower

Default Rate – refers to the average percentage of loans that are not repaid in accordance with the agreed-upon terms of a credit agreement in a given year

Delayed Draw (Term Loan) – a type of loan that allows a borrower to secure a loan commitment from a specified lender/group of lenders but delay the funding of the loan until a later date

Delever / Deleverage – to reduce the amount of debt outstanding of a borrower

Delinquent – refers to a borrower who has failed to make scheduled debt service payments on time

Discount Margin (DM) – represents the all-in spread over a base rate (LIBOR or SOFR) that a CLO Note will return assuming the CLO is not called early; made up of both the floating rate coupon of the Note as well as any discount that the CLO Note was purchased at, amortized over its remaining life

Diversity Score – a test that measures the diversification of the underlying loans in a CLO, taking into account the number of unique issuers and the industry sectors represented in the portfolio

EBITDA – a company's Earnings Before Interest, Taxes, Depreciation and Amortization; a proxy for annual cash generation

Excess CCC-Rated CLO – a broadly syndicated CLO in which the CCC maximum bucket is set to 17.5% rather than the usual 7.5%

Fee Rebate Letter - contract that entitles the CLO equity investor(s) to a portion of the CLO's management fees

First Lien – a creditor's legal claim or security interest that holds a first priority over all others claims or liens on the collateral of a borrower

Grace Period – a period of time after a debt service payment due date during which a borrower may be granted a temporary reprieve from making a payment without incurring late fees or penalties

High Yield Bond – fixed-rate debt security issued by companies with below investment grade credit ratings and/or limited credit history; carry higher interest rates to compensate investors for the increased risk of investing in these securities

Hurdle Rate – the minimum rate of return that an investment must earn for investors for a fund manager to be eligible to earn a performance or incentive fee

Illiquid – an asset or investment that cannot be easily and quickly converted to cash due to the asset's inherently limited trading activity or limited number of buyers

Incentive Fee - a performance-based fee that is paid to a fund manager or investment advisor when they generate returns on an investment that exceeds a certain benchmark or hurdle rate

Interest Coverage – the ratio of a borrower's EBITDA to its annual interest expense

Interest Coverage Test – in the context of a CLO, a test that measures the amount of interest received on the leveraged loans in comparison to the interest due on the CLO's notes

Internal Rate of Return (IRR) – a financial metric used to measure the profitability of an investment; the discount rate that makes the net present value of all cash flows equal to zero

Leveraged Buyout – a type of acquisition, typically by a private equity firm, in which a company is acquired using a large amount of debt financing

Leveraged Loan – a type of loan extended to companies perceived to be of lower credit quality or those that already have a considerable amount of debt

Leverage Multiple – the ratio of a borrower's debt outstanding, usually net of cash on the balance sheet, to its EBITDA

Liquid – an asset or investment that can be easily and quickly converted to cash due to the asset's frequent trading activity and a significant number of buyers

Loan-to-Value – the ratio of a borrower's debt outstanding to the estimated enterprise value of the entire business

London Interbank Offer Rate (LIBOR) – the benchmark interest rate at which major global banks lend to one another in the international interbank market for short-term loans; phased out in June of 2023

Loss Reserve – a discounting of the projected returns to the CLO equity by factoring in a default assumption

Management Discussion and Analysis – an analysis provided by the management team of a company to investors that details the company's financial performance, future business prospects, and potential risks or headwinds facing the business

Management Fee – a fee paid by an investor to a manager for managing their investment portfolio or assets

Margin Calls – a demand by a broker or lender for an investor to deposit additional funds or securities to cover losses

Mark-to-Market – a valuation process used to determine the current market value of a financial instrument or asset by comparing it to current market prices of similar instruments or assets

Market Value Over Collateral (MVOC) – the ratio of fair market value of underlying loans in a CLO + cash to the total balance of CLO notes in a specified tranche and those senior to that specified tranche

Net Asset Value (NAV) – represents the cash proceeds to the equity tranche if the CLO were liquidated on that date

Non-Call Period – a set period of time after a security is issued during which the issuer is prohibited from repaying the security

Overcollateralization Test – periodic test requiring the issuer of securities to maintain a minimum level of collateral in excess of the total amount of outstanding debt issued by the transaction

Paid-In-Kind (PIK) – a type of debt security that allows a borrower to accrue its interest expense to its outstanding debt balance rather than pay in cash

Par Build – an increase in the par balance of leveraged loans in a CLO

Par Burn – a decrease in par subordination of a CLO that can occur when levered loans default or if the CLO manager trades out of levered loans below the cost at which they were initially purchased

Par Flush – a payment to the CLO equity investor, usually capped at 0.5-1.0% of the CLO's par balance, that may occur if the CLO has built up excess loan portfolio par value shortly after issuance

Par Value – also called face value or nominal value, refers to the stated value of a financial instrument or security (i.e., the amount an issuer agrees to pay a creditor at maturity of a loan)

Prepayment – the payment of debt before its scheduled due date

Primary Market - the financial market in which investors can purchase newly-issued securities

Quality of Earnings – an analysis of a company's financial statements by a third-party accounting firm that assesses the sustainability and reliability of a company's reported earnings

Recovery Rate – the average percentage of defaulted loans that lenders recover through the bankruptcy process

Redemptions – refers to the process of investors selling their shares of a fund back to the investment company managing the fund

Reinvestment Period – a specified period during which the manager of a CLO can reinvest the cash flows received from the underlying loan portfolio into new loans

Reset – the process where the CLO's capital structure is adjusted to reflect changes in market conditions, such as changes in interest rates, credit spreads, or market volatility; requires making changes to all debt securities in the CLO

Return on Equity – a financial ratio that measures the profitability of a company or investment by calculating the amount of net income returned as a percentage of shareholder equity

Revolver / Revolving (Credit Facility) – a type of credit facility that allows a borrower to draw funds up to a predetermined amount and repay and redraw the funds again as needed

Sacred Rights Provision – a clause in a loan or bond agreement that protects lenders or bondholders by giving them the right to block or consent to certain actions taken by a borrower

Second Lien - First Lien – a creditor's legal claim or security interest that holds a second priority over all others' claims or liens on the borrower's collateral

Secondary Market – the financial market in which investors can buy and sell previously issued financial instruments from other investors rather than from the original issuer of the security

Secured Overnight Financing Rate (SOFR) – the interest rate at which institutions can borrow US dollars overnight while posting US Treasury first bonds as collateral

Sponsor – A private equity firm

Static CLO – a CLO that has no reinvestment period; each time a leverage loan prepays, the CLO will used the proceeds to pay down the CLO Notes

Synergies – refers to the benefits that arise from the combination or integration of two or more entities that can result in increased efficiency, cost savings, improved operations, and a stronger competitive position

Total Return Swaps – a financial contract in which two parties agree to exchange the total return of a particular asset or portfolio of assets over a specified period of time

Tranche – a specific portion of a CLO's capital structure with a given credit quality and risk-return profile

Tranche Thickness – This represents the percentage of the entire CLO that a specific tranche comprises

Trustee Report – a monthly report provided by the CLO trustee to the CLO investors that lists all the assets held by the CLO along with compliance test results and recent purchases and sales of loans

Volatility – the degree of variation or fluctuation in the value of a financial instrument over a period of time

Volcker Rule – a regulation that was implemented as part of the Dodd-Frank Wall Street Reform and Consumer Protection Act of 2010; prohibits banks from using their own funds to engage in risky trading activities that could put depositors' funds at risk

Waiver – an agreement between a lender and borrower that temporarily or permanently releases the borrower from certain obligations or requirements under the loan agreement

Waterfall – the order in which cash flows from the underlying assets are distributed to the different tranches of debt in a securitization

Weighted Average Life Test – a test that measures the weighted average amount of time it will take for the loans in the CLO's portfolio to be repaid

Weighted Average Rating Factor – a measure of the credit quality of the underlying portfolio of loans in a CLO that factors in the assigned credit rating of each loan in the portfolio and its respective principal balance

Weighted Average Spread Test – a test that measures the size and spread of each loan and ensures the weighted average of the portfolio meets a minimum required level

X Note – Highly rated note found in some CLOs w/ one-to-three-year scheduled amortization paid via cash flow that would have otherwise been paid to the CLO equity; commonly used in reset transactions

Yield – refers to the return generated by an investment over a specific period of time, typically expressed as a percentage of the initial investment